for the Love *of the* Sea

A cook book to celebrate the British seafood community and their food

Compiled by Jenny Jefferies

For the Love of the Sea

©2020 Jenny Jefferies & Meze Publishing Ltd. All rights reserved

First edition printed in 2021 in the UK

ISBN: 978-1-910863-75-6

Compiled by: Jenny Jefferies

Edited by: Katie Fisher, Phil Turner

Photography by: Paul Gregory, Simon Burt, Tim Green & Clair Irwin

Additional photography of Jenny: www.geoffreardon.com

Designed by: Paul Cocker

Contributors: Sarah Haworth, Michael Johnson, Lizzie Morton, Emma Toogood, Paul Stimpson

Printed in Great Britain by Bell and Bain Ltd, Glasgow

me:ze
PUBLISHING

Published by Meze Publishing Limited
Unit 1b, 2 Kelham Square
Kelham Riverside
Sheffield S3 8SD
Web: www.mezepublishing.co.uk
Telephone: 0114 275 7709
Email: info@mezepublishing.co.uk

FOREWORD

BY MARCUS COLEMAN, CEO, SEAFISH

Over the years, seafood has been viewed as a food source that possessed mystical powers; oysters in particular, it is claimed, helped legendary 18th century lover Casanova.

Whether or not there is any truth in those claims is probably best left to others, but here I want to acknowledge passions of a different kind; those that so many working in the seafood industry have for their heritage, their communities, their businesses and, of course, the wonderful seafood they bring to homes and restaurants throughout the United Kingdom.

There are around 12,000 commercial fishermen in the UK and Seafish aim to give the industry the support it needs to thrive. When I meet fishermen and women, many will proudly talk about their fishing roots: fathers, grandfathers, continuing the family tradition. It is a dangerous profession and one that sadly claims lives every year. The hostile working environment is very unforgiving, yet the drive to battle the elements and deliver the catch to the quayside urges them on.

Nearly half a million tonnes of seafood is landed at ports all around the UK every year, from Newlyn in south west Cornwall to Lerwick in the Shetland Islands. Fish markets bring out another passion; an early morning clamour to do the best deal, to get the right prices. Traditional 'shout auctions' are pure theatre.

The merchants in turn distribute the catch to seafood processing businesses - over 350 around the UK employing 20,000+ people - often located in rural coastal communities. These jobs are essential to many communities and from here, the supermarkets, restaurants, workplaces and good old fish and chip shops receive their supplies and proudly assemble a wonderful array of seafood options for UK consumers. There is so much to choose from; the waters around the UK yield such a wide variety of species.

As an island nation, we have a deep relationship with the sea around us, but in recent years, our eating habits have sometimes overlooked the wonderful variety of seafood available in Britain. Here at Seafish we help support companies throughout the seafood supply chain and we ourselves are passionate about turning the tide to encourage the great British public to once again fall in love with seafood.

Marcus Coleman, CEO, Seafish

CONTENTS

PREFACE

· ·

BY JENNY JEFFERIES

Fishing is the most dangerous peacetime occupation, and all men and women in the industry should be acknowledged and respected. Their traditions, passion and dedication are found throughout these stories and recipes that come from the cold seas to our warm kitchen tables. Each one takes you on a journey through the British Isles, to places up and down the country where fishing is the lifeblood.

I hope this book helps to give thanks and praise to everyone who loves British seafood and works with the sea in whatever form, from fishing and farming to selling, cooking, preparing, managing, researching and recreationally. I also hope this book fairly represents the female voice within the British seafood industry; 90% of the people involved in the processing are women, 54% of the entire workforce are women and more women than ever before are going out to sea.

For the Love of the Sea champions sustainability, highlights aquaculture and shares the aspirations of British fishermen and women, wholesalers, fishmongers, chefs, hoteliers, restaurateurs, scientists and researchers, sailors, artists and many more besides.

There is a real emotive sense of tradition, history and accomplishment throughout this book that gives the stories and accompanying images lovely credibility and grace.

We are so lucky to live on an island that enjoys such a diverse array of food. Let's embrace that while protecting nature and thinking of our future generations.

It's been a huge privilege and an immense joy putting this book together, following For the Love of the Land which also celebrates British produce. As farmers are the custodians of the countryside, fishermen are the gatekeepers of the sea.

Many thanks to all our contributors plus Marcus Coleman, Phil Turner, Paul Cocker, Katie Fisher, Emma Toogood, Paul Gregory, Simon Burt, Claire Irwin, Tim Green, Geoff Reardon, Emilie Silverwood-Cope, my husband John and my two daughters Heidi and Florence.

A proportion of my profits from For the Love of the Sea will be donated to the RNLI.*

Enjoy!

Jenny Jefferies (www.jennyjefferies.co.uk)

*22% of the net profits will be paid in support of the RNLI. Payments are made to RNLI (Sales) Ltd (which pays all its taxable profits to the RNLI, a charity registered in England and Wales (209603), Scotland (SC037736), the Republic of Ireland (20003326), the Bailiwick of Jersey (14), the Isle of Man and the Bailiwick of Guernsey and Alderney, of West Quay Road, Poole, Dorset BH15 1HZ).

AMY O'BRIEN

"I'd like to see Cornish fish stocked in supermarkets more often; a lot of their stock comes from overseas and we should be encouraging British people to get into British fish."

I've always enjoyed being at sea, and worked on private yachts in the south of France from the age of 21. I came home to Newlyn in 2019 for some family time, and was due to go back the following year but of course the coronavirus pandemic put a complete stop to that. It didn't take long for me to get bored of being on land though, so I started bugging skippers I knew to take me out to sea. Luckily one of them did, and I picked up the necessary skills very fast so he offered me a job. For me, being at sea and at home in Cornwall has been an absolute revelation and there's nothing better than watching a sunset or sunrise on the water.

We go to sea most evenings to fish with a ring-netting vessel, which uses a net to encircle the fish and bring them on board. Our targets are mainly sardines and anchovies, which we supply to a local fishery who sort and sell them on. Unfortunately, anchovies are hardly worth anything at the moment, but I love them and so does my dad so a lot get brought home and eaten! We often swap some of our catch in the harbour as well; I love monkfish and mackerel so other fishermen will sometimes trade those. I'd like to see Cornish fish stocked in supermarkets more often; a lot of their stock comes from overseas and we should be encouraging British people to get into British fish. It would be so much more popular if it was always incredibly fresh and readily available, like you find at the fishmongers round here.

Sardines aren't particularly popular in the UK either unless they're tinned, and even that process actually happens in France and Spain because there aren't any factories left in Cornwall (the nearest was already a museum when I was growing up!). It's such a shame because they're amazing fish and incredibly versatile to cook with: baked, breadcrumbed, barbecued...I think the bones put people off but you can buy them butterflied which makes them so easy to eat. All the sardines round here are caught by our fleet of 15 boats, which belongs to the Cornish Sardine Management Association. This means they must be under 15 metres and only fish within a set limit from the shore, as all Cornish fishermen want to protect our stocks for the future.

Photos © Sam Breeze

LEMON COCONUT DHAL WITH MONKFISH AND SAMPHIRE

· ·

I picked up this recipe when travelling around Sri Lanka in 2017. It has become a favourite dish to make for friends and family and I now always have the basic ingredients in the cupboard. I have adapted it over time to work with ingredients local to Cornwall, like monkfish and samphire which I think complement it wonderfully! –
Amy O'Brien

Sunflower or vegetable oil

1 ½ large white onions or 3-4 big shallots, finely chopped

5 large cloves of garlic, very finely chopped or minced

2 thumbs of fresh ginger, minced (or 1 tbsp ground ginger)

2 green chillies, finely chopped

1 tbsp mild or medium curry powder

2 tbsp ground fenugreek

1 tsp ground turmeric (for colour, not essential)

500g red lentils

2 tins of coconut milk

1 tin of chopped tomatoes

3 large lemons, juiced

Cornish sea salt

Freshly ground black pepper

1 monkfish tail, boneless and cut into chunks (approx. 600-800g)

1 large thumb of Cornish butter

400g samphire

Put a large, preferably non-stick saucepan with a lid on a low heat and add a glug of oil. Add the chopped onions and put the lid on to soften them for 5 minutes or more. Do not brown. When the onions are soft, add the garlic, ginger, chillies, curry powder, fenugreek and turmeric, if using. Cook for another 5 minutes, stirring continuously.

Rinse the lentils under cold running water, drain well, then add them to the pan along with the coconut milk. Mix everything together, then turn the heat up a little and leave the dhal to cook with the lid on, stirring occasionally. Fill one of the empty tins with water if you've used particularly thick coconut milk and add this to the pan. It may need more water later, but use your own judgement as the chopped tomatoes and lemon juice will add liquid too and you don't want a runny dhal.

After the dhal has been cooking for about 30 minutes, add the chopped tomatoes. The lentils should take about 40 minutes to cook, but have a taste at this point to see if they have softened up. When the lentils are done, stir in the lemon juice, add salt and pepper to taste, mix well and allow the dhal to rest on a low heat.

Heat a little oil in a frying pan and cook the monkfish until done to your liking, then set aside. In the same frying pan, melt the butter and sauté the samphire with a little salt. Ladle the dhal into 4 dishes and place the monkfish and samphire on top to serve.

This recipe also works well with pan fried Cornish mackerel fillets, grilled squid or tiger prawns. If you want a more hearty vegan dish, swap the monkfish for sweet potato and spinach, and use oil instead of butter. You'll probably have enough leftover dhal for lunch or dinner the next day when all the spices and flavours have matured; curry is ALWAYS better the next day!

PREPARATION TIME: 20 MINUTES | COOKING TIME: I HOUR | SERVES 4

ASHTON FISHMONGERS

BY NICK ADAMS

"We've built up a reputation as one of the leading suppliers of fish and seafood in the UK and are proud to be such a longstanding, independent, family-owned business."

We're a family business, run by myself and my brother Jonathan who is the managing director. In 1973, our late father John bought the business from Douglas Ashton whose family had owned the fishmongers for many decades previously, hence the name, but it actually dates back to the year 1800 when Edmund and Mary Ward established the original fishmongers and game dealers. The business has only changed hands twice in all that time, over 200 years, and Ashton's is one of the oldest limited companies in Cardiff as well as one of the largest independent fishmongers in the UK.

Today, we employ about 25 people and sell many different varieties of fish and shellfish, as well as game including pheasant, wild duck and wild boar and exotic meats such as zebra, camel, crocodile and kangaroo. Our stall in Cardiff Central Market is open six days a week, and we pride ourselves on the quality and freshness of the fish we sell as well as the fantastic displays created by our experienced fishmongers. Three of them have won the British Fish Craft Championships while working for us: Michael Crates, who's been here for nearly 50 years now; Kevin Todd; and Nick Wood.

Our fresh produce comes from all over the UK including ports in Devon, Cornwall, Lowestoft, Hull, Grimsby, Aberdeen and Fleetwood. Unfortunately, most of the catch from Wales itself goes to Spain and Portugal; it's all down to the lack of an integrated transport system here. We'd love to sell Welsh fish and seafood, but we try to make the most of other British suppliers. The market stall will typically have the usual species like cod, haddock, hake, salmon, plaice and sea bass alongside several overseas options such as tuna, and the shellfish selection includes lobsters, crabs, clams, mussels, many different types of prawns and more. We also sell fresh laverbread, a Welsh delicacy that can be hard to find elsewhere, and can ship it to customers anywhere in the British Isles.

Alongside the public in Cardiff, we supply restaurants and hotels across south Wales with top quality produce, as far west as Swansea, up to Abergavenny and in the Newport area too. We've built up a reputation as one of the leading suppliers of fish and seafood in the UK and are proud to be such a longstanding, independent, family-owned business.

THAI-STYLE PRAWN AND NOODLE SOUP

This delicious meal is light yet full of flavour. Shellfish such as prawns go very well with spicy and aromatic ingredients like the chillies, ginger and lemongrass used here. Be careful not to overcook the prawns as it spoils their texture. — Nick Adams

1 tbsp sunflower oil

1 onion, chopped

2 small green chillies, deseeded and finely chopped

2.5cm piece of fresh root ginger, peeled and chopped

50g mixed mushrooms (such as shiitake, oyster, chestnut and button)

2 litres fish or vegetable stock

2 tbsp rice wine or white wine vinegar

1 lemongrass stalk, peeled and chopped

455g large cooked and peeled prawns (fresh or defrosted)

115g rice noodles

4 tbsp chopped fresh coriander

Spring onions, finely sliced

Heat the oil in a large saucepan, then put the onion, chillies and ginger in to cook for 2 minutes. Add the mushrooms and cook for 3 minutes, stirring occasionally.

Pour in the stock and rice wine or white wine vinegar. Add the chopped lemongrass, bring the broth to the boil and then simmer for 10 to 12 minutes.

Add the prawns, noodles and coriander then bring the soup back to the boil. Reduce the heat and simmer for 3 to 4 minutes.

Divide the ingredients and broth evenly between 4 bowls, then serve the prawn and noodle soup garnished with the finely sliced spring onions.

PREPARATION TIME: 10 MINUTES | COOKING TIME: 20-25 MINUTES | SERVES 4

BALLY PHILP

"I would like to see people be more discerning about where and how their seafood is produced, and encourage people wherever possible to look for creel-caught and hand-dived shellfish, preferably caught locally by small scale fishing boats."

I have been a fisherman for over 30 years, and much of that time has been spent working a creel boat from the Isle of Skye. I am passionate about promoting sustainable fisheries and reversing decades of poor government management of our inshore fisheries.

I work part-time for the Scottish Creel Fishermen's Federation, and we are members of the OURSEAS coalition who are promoting sustainable fisheries. We are also fighting hard for the reintroduction of a coastal limit on where trawling and dredging are allowed to be used.

I would like to see people be more discerning about where and how their seafood is produced, and encourage people wherever possible to look for creel-caught and hand-dived shellfish, preferably caught locally by small scale fishing boats.

Like all food production, there is a range of standards available and by demanding local and sustainably caught seafood wherever possible, we end up with the best quality seafood on our plates while playing our part in promoting sustainable fisheries.

Thankfully in Scotland we still have access to some of the best seafood in the world. If we look after our seas and our inshore fishermen, this will continue for generations to come.

If you are ever in the Isle of Skye area, look us up! We regularly land the day's catch into the harbour in the village of Kyleakin, and are happy to supply small quantities of prawns and langoustines for cash sales (there's no card reader aboard, sorry!). We are not out fishing every day though, so give us as much notice as possible and we will try to save you some of Scotland's best shellfish to enjoy.

Photos © Kyla Orr

PRAWN AND SQUAT LOBSTER CURRY

Squat lobsters are not actually lobsters, but a species of shellfish similar to small crabs. They're relatively common in Scottish waters but tend not to be available elsewhere, so you can just use prawns if needed. If you can find prepared tails though, they make a flavoursome addition to this warming curry. – Bally Philp

4 tbsp vegetable oil

2 onions, sliced

2 chillies, sliced

6 cloves of garlic, sliced

2 tsp ground turmeric

2 tsp garam masala

2 tsp chilli powder

1 tsp ground coriander

1 tsp ground cumin

1 tsp ground ginger

3 medium tomatoes, quartered

2 tins of chopped tomatoes

500g prawns and squat tails, boiled and shelled

Small bunch of fresh coriander, chopped

Place a large pan on a medium-high heat, add 2 tablespoons of the vegetable oil and wait until it gets hot.

Put the sliced onions and chillies into the pan and fry until the onions are translucent. Add the sliced garlic, the remaining oil and all the spices. Cook until everything is browned and aromatic.

Add the quartered tomatoes to the pan and fry until the moisture frees the spices from the bottom of the pan, then add the tinned tomatoes. Turn the heat down low and simmer the sauce for 10 to 15 minutes.

Lastly, add the prepared prawns and squat tails along with the chopped coriander. Stir everything together and taste to check the seasoning. The curry is now ready to serve with boiled rice.

PREPARATION TIME: 15 MINUTES | COOKING TIME: APPROX. 45 MINUTES | SERVES 4

CÂR-Y-MÔR

BY MEGAN HAINES

"As a Community Benefit Society, our main aim is to benefit local people and businesses. Here in St David's, local fishermen, boat builders and other caring folk have all joined the society to start creating an innovative seafood business providing fulfilling jobs."

Câr-Y-Môr started through a combined passion for the coast and a desire to have a positive impact on people's health and wellbeing. It has been a long road to get where we are today! As a Community Benefit Society, our main aim is to benefit local people and businesses. Here in St David's, local fishermen, boat builders and other caring folk have all joined the society to start creating an innovative seafood business providing fulfilling jobs. Today the society has 37 members and counting: all local members volunteering to help the community business grow, with others supporting from afar.

2020 was a big year for us as we finally managed to get Wales' first 3D ocean farms into the water at Ramsey Sound, Pembrokeshire. Between the two ocean farms we have three different species of seaweed growing and 90,000 juvenile native oysters. By spring 2021 we hope to settle wild mussel seed. Surveying the farms and seeing the magic that happens has brought us and our partners great joy, especially during these turbulent times. But as well as boosting our collective mood, the farms will also be used by our many research partners for a number of interesting studies: evaluating the positive effect they have on the marine environment, exploring carbon capture potential and the development of a farm monitoring system.

Back on land we have allied with Jono and Sandy at Solva Seafoods, which allows us to market and distribute locally caught seafood and shellfish to local and national customers, supplying them with lobster and crab caught by Jono himself. As the business develops, we hope to increase this offer with more locally caught and ocean farmed produce.

In the summer of 2019, we began our adventure into outdoor education, meaning you would find us most weekends on different beaches across southern Pembrokeshire. Our Seaweed Potion Kitchen proved particularly popular with both children and adults (as it meant parents could have five minutes' peace!). We also delved into doing education sessions in schools as well as running Potion Kitchen birthday parties on the beach, all of which were a fantastic success and a joy to be part of.

As Câr-Y-Môr moves forward, we hope to carry on inspiring the next generation of ocean farmers, to continue bringing something special to the local community and really make a positive difference to people's wellbeing here.

GRILLED LOBSTER WITH LAVER AND GARLIC BUTTER

This is a real showstopper and a perfect meal to serve on a summer's evening with everyone gathered around the barbecue. — Billy Trigg.

1 lobster

30g Welsh cheddar

For the laver butter

100g salted butter, softened

10g dried laver

3 cloves of garlic

5g fresh parsley

5g fresh coriander

Place the live lobster in the freezer for 10 minutes. This will put the lobster into a coma-like state. In the meantime, grate the cheddar and blend all the ingredients for the laver butter together in a food processor.

After 10 minutes, remove the lobster from the freezer, place it on a chopping board and cut through the lobster's head quickly with a very sharp knife, as this causes as little pain as possible. Cut the lobster in half lengthways and remove the digestive tract. Crack the shell of the claws with the back of your knife.

Spread the laver butter then sprinkle the cheese over the lobster meat and claws. Place under a preheated grill or on a hot barbecue for 20 minutes until cooked but tender.

Serve the lobster with homemade chunky chips and a summer salad, garnished with a slice of lemon or lime.

PREPARATION TIME: 15 MINUTES | COOKING TIME: 20 MINUTES | SERVES 2

COLMAN'S OF SOUTH SHIELDS

BY RICHARD COLMAN ORD

"Fish and chips and seafood have been at the forefront of our family for five generations now, and the pleasure we get from serving such amazing produce to our customers is what makes us so proud to keep on doing what we do."

Colman's is our family business which has been owned and operated by our family since 1905! We started out as a small wooden hut on the beach, and progressed to where we are today. We are passionate about what we do, and sustainability is at the heart of our ethos; it's important that future generations can enjoy the dishes we are all so used to. Fish and chips and seafood have been at the forefront of our family for five generations now, and the pleasure we get from serving such amazing produce to our customers is what makes us so proud to keep on doing what we do.

Our fish and chip restaurant and takeaway on Ocean Road was established in 1926 and remains in the same location today (although we've knocked through a few buildings next door!). During this time, four generations of my family have worked in this premises to build it up to what it is today. Our fish and chips have attracted a huge following over the years from Sting to Patrick Stewart, and Tony Blair to Sam Mendes... the list goes on, and we also proudly cooked for the Queen's birthday parties at the embassies in Rome and Guatemala.

Our Seafood Temple opened in 2017, just in front of where our original hut was situated back in 1905, so we've gone back to where it all began! We restored an old bandstand formally known to the locals as 'Gandhi's Temple' which was built in 1931, and from there extended the restaurant towards the beach to give unrivalled panoramic sea views. In the bandstand itself we have a cocktail and oyster bar serving the fantastic local Lindisfarne oysters.

Where Colman's on Ocean Road is our traditional restaurant, serving the nation's favourite fish and chips in all its glory, our Seafood Temple showcases the amazing fish and seafood that our north east coast has to offer, supporting all the local fishermen along the way. Our casual family dining approach means that everyone can enjoy fish and seafood, and see for themselves why we believe the north east coast has some of the best fish and seafood in the world!

Photos © Andy Gibbins Images, House of Hues, Steven Lomas, Tim Green

COLMAN'S CLASSIC COD AND CHIPS

....

At Colman's, we have been serving our fish and chips for over 100 years, and even cooking them at the Queen's birthday parties! We thought we would share our knowledge so you can give this recipe a go at home. – Richard Colman Ord

4 cod fillets, each weighing around 170-180g (choose MSC sustainable fish where possible)

100g plain flour, seasoned

For the batter

220g plain flour

275ml cold water

5g salt

25ml malt vinegar

3g bicarbonate of soda

For the chips

6 potatoes (Maris Pipers if available)

1.5 litres vegetable oil (sunflower is best)

To make the perfect fish and chips, you need to start by buying the right fish. Ensure that the fish is as fresh as possible and try to buy sustainable fish wherever possible. Look out for the MSC blue fish logo!

For the batter

Combine all the ingredients in a bowl and whisk until smooth. The batter needs to be a similar consistency to single cream. You may need to add a little bit more flour or water to get the desired consistency. Once the batter is ready, chill in the fridge for at least 45 minutes.

For the chips

Peel the potatoes and cut them into evenly-sized batons that aren't too thin. Wash under cold water to remove any starch and drain well.

We cook the chips in two stages to get a soft, fluffy centre and a crisp outside! First, heat the oil in a deep fat fryer to 130°c. Fry the chips for 7 to 8 minutes until soft. Lift out of the oil and drain.

Reheat the oil to 180°c and return the chips to the pan, cooking until they are crispy and brown. Drain well. Keep in a warm place while you cook the fish.

Set the deep fat fryer to 180°c. Lightly coat the cod fillets in the seasoned plain flour and pat off. Dip in the batter and allow most of the batter to run off the fish as it only has to be lightly coated. Make sure the batter is nice and cold. Hot oil and cold batter = perfect crispiness!

Hold each fillet halfway into the oil for a few seconds before lowering it gently away from you to avoid splashing the oil. If you let go straight away it will sink to the bottom and stick.

The fish should take approximately 4 to 5 minutes to cook. Ensure the batter is golden and crisp before removing and draining thoroughly on kitchen paper. Keep the cooked fish warm in a low oven while you cook the remaining fish in the same way.

Serve the fish and chips with salt and vinegar, tartare sauce and a wedge of lemon!

PREPARATION TIME: I HOUR | COOKING TIME: 30-45 MINUTES | SERVES 4

THE CORNISH SEAWEED COMPANY

BY CAROLINE WARWICK-EVANS

"In the future, we expect to harvest more from the farms and less from the wild to ensure the sustainability of our seaweed stocks. Our hope is that seaweed becomes more understood as the incredible resource it is, and that people embrace learning about how to cook with it."

The Cornish Seaweed Company was established in 2012 after I heard a radio program early one morning about the seaweed industry in Ireland, and realised that there was no such industry in England. I had just returned from many years working and travelling overseas, and my good friend Tim van Berkel, a conservationist, was also looking for work while running a charity but working as a waiter to pay the bills. When I asked if he would be keen to start the first seaweed company in Cornwall with me, he jumped at the idea!

Things moved pretty quickly from there; Tim and I volunteered at a seaweed company on the west coast of Ireland in exchange for training, learning to understand the different species as well as how to harvest and process them. Back in Cornwall, we navigated through the complex red tape surrounding coastal ownership, oversight and food standards authorities to really begin the journey. The following few years saw us working flat out, living on very little and in caravans: I can safely say that I would not relive this time ever again!

However, after many years of struggling, seaweed suddenly leapt into the limelight and seemed to become the most talked-about superfood on the planet, much to our happiness and relief! Celebrity chefs from Jamie Oliver to Heston Blumenthal started to get in touch with us and place orders, so the business was able to grow. Eight years down the line, we supply mainstream supermarkets as well as restaurants, health food stores and delis and even have competition from other seaweed companies following in our wake. Our own publication, The Seaweed Cookbook, is still flying off the shelves and we are developing new products regularly.

Our team has grown to consist of a wonderful group of passionate individuals which makes a hard day's work a lot of fun, and we are very grateful for this. We harvest the seaweed by free diving in the crystal clear waters around west Cornwall from our boat, and recently deployed our first lines for growing our own seaweeds in an offshore farm. In the future, we expect to harvest more from the farms and less from the wild to ensure the sustainability of our seaweed stocks. Our hope is that seaweed becomes more understood as the incredible resource it is, and that people embrace learning about how to cook with it. Let the journey continue!

GARLICKY SEA SPAGHETTI TAGLIATELLE WITH CRISPY DULSE

....

This is my go-to seaweed recipe as it offers a wonderfully simple yet exciting introduction to the world of seaweed cooking. Classified as a superfood and bursting with vitamins and minerals, sea spaghetti is a great option for the whole family and can be added to any pasta dish. — Caroline Warwick-Evans

Olive oil

8 cloves of garlic, finely chopped

Selection of fresh seasonal greens, chopped (such as cavalo nero, kale, rocket, spinach)

350g tagliatelle (optional: wholewheat)

30g dried organic Cornish Seaweed Sea Spaghetti

40g dried organic Cornish Seaweed Dulse

1 lemon, cut into wedges

Organic Seaweed Salt and Pepper

75g parmesan, grated

25g fresh parsley, chopped

25g fresh coriander, chopped

Heat a glug of olive oil in a frying pan and add the garlic to fry on a low heat. Stir in the chopped greens (except rocket, if using) and cook for a few minutes, then set aside.

Meanwhile, bring a pan of water to the boil with some salt and oil. Add the tagliatelle and organic sea spaghetti and cook for 8 to 10 minutes.

For the crispy dulse, put the oven on a low heat. Cut the dulse into 8 to 10cm pieces with scissors and arrange on a baking tray. Toast on a low heat for 2 to 3 minutes. Be careful not to burn them! Remove from the oven and leave to cool.

Drain the pasta and sea spaghetti and return them to the pan. Toss the garlicky greens in (including the rocket, if using) and mix gently with a drizzle of extra oil, plenty of freshly squeezed lemon juice and seasoning.

To serve

Crumble the toasted crispy dulse over the top, scatter over the parmesan and serve with plenty of fresh herbs, extra lemon and pepper.

PREPARATION TIME: 10 MINUTES | COOKING TIME: 10 MINUTES | SERVES 4

CRASTER KIPPERS

BY NEIL ROBSON

"I'm the fourth generation of my family to smoke this world famous delicacy, using smokehouses that were built in 1856 and the traditional methods first employed by my great-grandfather, which have been passed down through generations over the centuries."

Kippers have been smoked in the small village of Craster, perched on the Northumbrian coast, for over 150 years. I'm the fourth generation of my family to smoke this world famous delicacy, using smokehouses that were built in 1856 and the traditional methods first employed by my great-grandfather, which have been passed down through generations over the centuries.

I've seen massive changes in the industry during my tenure of the business, L. Robson & Sons. These include new regulations around food safety, which I welcomed and embraced, to the sourcing of our raw materials, the 'silver darlings' that are North Sea herring. At one time, these fish were landed in the small harbour just a few yards away from the smokehouse, but overfishing and a total ban of the landing of herring meant they had to be sourced from further afield, initially from Scotland but more recently from Norway. All our herring are MSC approved which means they are caught from a responsibly managed fishery to enable the long term future and sustainability of the herring fishery.

The process we then follow is very simple. First, the herring are split down their backs on a machine capable of processing 500kg of fish per hour, which replaces the numerous 'herring girls' that used to do the job by hand. Next, the herring are placed in a brine solution for a predetermined length of time depending on their size. Lastly, they are hung on tenter hooks and placed in the cavernous smokehouses.

In the smokehouses, fires are placed under the rows of prepared herring, made of whitewood shavings and oak sawdust, and these smoulder away for up to 16 hours. This is where the skill of the smoker takes place, as the oak smoke changes the herrings into golden kippers. After the transformation has taken place, the kippers are packed for dispatch throughout the UK. Our products are available at Waitrose supermarkets across the country, and customers can also order directly from our website.

I think of myself as the mere custodian of this family business, and look forward to passing it over to my daughters, Olivia and Georgia, so they can carry on the family tradition of producing Craster Kippers.

CRASTER KIPPER CLUB SANDWICH

....

This is comfort food at its best. Our smoked kipper has such an authentic, traditional flavour, perfected over five generations and enjoyed globally. We feel it's most satisfying when served simply. This sandwich is especially rewarding after a brisk coastal stroll with a cup of our Craster Harbour tea, or served on a summer deck with a crisp white burgundy. — Neil Robson

4 Craster Kipper fillets

1 tbsp butter

4 eggs

6 romaine lettuce leaves (crunchy is best)

1 ripe avocado

4 tbsp mayonnaise

1 lemon, juiced

Black pepper

8 slices of good quality brown bread (rye sourdough or Irish soda bread work well)

Place the kipper fillets in a piece of foil with the butter. Seal to make a parcel and cook in a hot oven, under a grill or on a barbecue for 4 to 6 minutes until hot throughout.

Meanwhile, put the eggs in a pan of boiling water for 4 to 5 minutes. Wash and finely shred the lettuce, peel and slice the avocado. Mix the mayonnaise with the lemon juice and some black pepper to taste in a cup. When the eggs are done, shell and slice or chop them to your liking.

Pile the lettuce and avocado onto four slices of the bread, dividing them equally. Skin the hot buttered kipper fillets and place on top, pouring the melted butter over the fish. Next, add a layer of boiled egg. Finally, slather the lemon mayo over the remaining four slices of bread and top your creation off to make four sandwiches. Eat while the juices are still hot.

DEE CAFFARI MBE

"Many of us consider fish and seafood a treat, or perhaps a dish that we tend to eat more when we are abroad. British seafood is not only a healthy choice but, if managed properly, can be a sustainable choice too."

Having spent the majority of my career sailing seas around the world, I have been fortunate enough to have experienced and enjoyed some beautiful coastlines. In 2006 I became the first woman to sail solo around the world the wrong way, non-stop. Following my 6th place finish in the Vendée Globe 2008/9, I entered the record books once again to become the first woman to sail solo and non-stop around the globe in both directions. As skipper of 'Turn the Tide on Plastic' - a mixed, youth focused team with a strong sustainability message – I completed my sixth lap of the planet on the Volvo Ocean Race 2017/18.

One of my greatest pleasures, however, is sailing my home waters on the south coast of Britain. As an island nation, our coastline is rich with resources and the UK is a key exporter of fish and seafood to the rest of the world. In light of this, I have always found it strange that the perception of other nations, and one that we are judged on, is our traditional fare of greasy fish and chips. Although the reality of British seafood is so much more than this, many of us consider fish and seafood a treat, or perhaps a dish that we tend to eat more when we are abroad. Seafood is not only a healthy choice but, if managed properly, can be a sustainable choice too.

However, seafood is facing two serious issues. The first is sustainability. We must balance our consumption to ensure stocks are maintained; the Marine Stewardship Council are offering little blue labels on fish that are caught sustainably so that consumers can make decisions that protect the big blue into the future. The second issue, which I feel extremely passionate about, is plastic pollution and its impact on the food we consume. There has been a concerted effort to reduce single-use plastic in our daily lives as we have all been shocked and horrified by the amount that ends up in our oceans, broken down into micro plastics and ingested by sea life.

We all need to take steps to avoid the threat of overfishing and plastic contamination to protect the health of our seas and oceans. I love seafood and would encourage everyone to shop local, support our fishermen and keep our oceans healthy for future generations to enjoy.

clean seas
turn the tide
on plastic

FISH PIE

· ·

This recipe is a perfect winter warmer and ideal when cooking for people with slightly different tastes, because they can choose between parsley and cheese sauce!
— Dee Caffari

1kg potatoes for mashing, peeled and halved

25g butter

25g plain flour

4 spring onions, finely sliced

400ml milk

1 tsp Dijon mustard

Small bunch of fresh parsley, finely chopped

50g cheddar, grated, plus extra to sprinkle over the top of the pie

400g cod, cubed

Salt and pepper, to taste

Spring onions, chopped (optional)

Preheat the oven to 200°c/180°c fan/Gas Mark 6. Put the peeled and halved potatoes in a saucepan of water. Bring to the boil then reduce the heat to a simmer until they are tender.

Meanwhile, put the butter and plain flour into another pan with the finely sliced spring onions. Heat gently until the butter has melted, stirring regularly. Cook for 1 to 2 minutes until you have a smooth paste. Gradually whisk in the milk, using a balloon whisk if you have one. Bring the sauce to the boil, stirring continuously to avoid any lumps and sticking on the bottom of the pan. Cook for 3 to 4 minutes until thickened.

Take the pan off the heat and stir the mustard into the sauce before pouring half of it into another saucepan. Add the chopped parsley to one saucepan. Add the grated cheese to the other half of the sauce, then return this pan to the heat to gently melt the cheese.

Mix half the cod pieces into the parsley sauce and the other half into the cheese sauce. Spoon the fillings into an ovenproof dish, parsley sauce at one end and cheese sauce at the other.

When the potatoes are cooked, drain and mash them with a splash of milk and a knob of butter. Season the mash to taste with salt and pepper, then spoon it over the fish pie filling and sprinkle the top with a handful of grated cheddar cheese.

Place the pie in the preheated oven for 20 to 25 minutes, or until golden and bubbling at the edges. If you like, sprinkle some chopped spring onion over the pie to decorate before serving.

DEE CAFFARI MBE

· ·

PAGE 46

PREPARATION TIME: 15 MINUTES | COOKING TIME: 50-55 MINUTES | SERVES 4

THE FEMALE FISHERMAN

BY ASHLEY MULLENGER

"The hours are long and often unsociable, the job can be hard on your body with hours outside in the cold, wind and rain, but I adore it. Maybe it's the complete honesty of the job: a fair day's work for a fair day's pay."

I own and operate two boats working from Wells-next-the-Sea which is a small seaside town on the north Norfolk coast. My traditional Scottish-built boat, Fairlass, predominantly catches whelks, while the smaller 8m fibreglass boat Saoirse catches crabs and lobsters too. It's no secret that this has historically been a man's job, and as a 'female fisherman' I am often asked 'how did that happen?' Occasionally I will find myself staring down at a box full of stinking bait, splattered with mud, rain streaming down my face at some god awful time of the night, wondering the same thing! I wouldn't change the decision I made to ditch the clean, warm office life for a second though.

In 2009 I decided to book myself on a charter angling trip from Wells, and I fell in love with being at sea. The skipper, Nigel, couldn't get rid of me afterwards so eventually he asked me to work with him. I spent my summers gutting mackerel and cod and wrestling the odd small shark until 2013, when Nigel sold Sunbeam III and started fishing commercially before buying his own boat, Never Can Tell-A.

Despite desperately wanting to have a career at sea, I was always put off by the level of physical work involved, the danger and the fact that commercial day boats don't generally cater for female needs. However, in 2018 Nigel asked me to come back and work for him again, and I've never looked back. The hours are long and often unsociable, the job can be hard on your body with hours outside in the cold, wind and rain, but I adore it. Maybe it's the complete honesty of the job: a fair day's work for a fair day's pay. Maybe it's the romance of working with nature and the elements? I try not to analyse it but just appreciate how lucky I am.

We retired Never Can Tell-A in 2019 and replaced her with Fairlass, which Nigel's sons predominantly run. Saoirse joined the fleet in October 2020 and we hope to diversify our catch with her, including fish in the longer term to sell locally. I am deeply passionate about fish caught in the UK and would love to see the British public seeking out more of our own 'home-grown' fish, so that we don't have to rely as heavily on exporting our catch abroad.

CRAB DIP

· ·

This is a real crowd pleaser, and a great way to introduce people to brown crab if they haven't eaten it before. It's easy to make ahead of time and reheat for entertaining. Try to find the best locally sourced brown crab you can for great quality and to support local fishermen. — Ashley Mullenger, The Female Fisherman

1 large dressed brown crab

180g cream cheese

6 spring onions, finely sliced

5 tbsp mayonnaise

2 cloves of garlic, finely minced (or 1 tsp garlic powder)

1 tsp Worcestershire sauce

½ tsp paprika

Salt, pepper and Tabasco to taste

Good handful of grated cheddar or mozzarella

Set aside half of the grated cheese, then put all the ingredients into a large bowl. Combine until well mixed, then spoon into individual ovenproof bowls or one larger dish for sharing.

Bake the dip in a preheated oven at 180°c for 20 minutes, then take it out and turn on the grill. Scatter the remaining grated cheese over the top of the dip, then grill until golden.

Leave the dip to cool slightly before serving. This is ideal with fresh bread, toasted pittas, crackers, tortilla chips or even celery and cucumber sticks.

FISHERMAN'S FRIENDS

BY JON CLEAVE

"Over the years, our Friday nights down by the harbour, singing about ships and storms and sailors and, yes, fish, became a popular tradition in Port Isaac with locals and visitors alike."

It was thirty years ago that Caroline and I embarked on our voyage, bound for North Cornwall, back to Port Isaac. We'd decided to take on the old lifeboat house, perched on the very edge of the harbour, and turn it into a shop filled with every hue of nauticalia. We still live in that same village, in an old Captain's house where we had our three sons. Jacob, George and Theo would run down to the beach and spend barefoot and sandy days rockpooling and swimming in the best playground any child could ever have; the very same one that I'd had as a boy, and always with the ever-changing grandeur of the Atlantic Ocean as backdrop. As it had been with me, the sea became a part of them.

Soon after I'd returned to Cornwall, I began to sing with a few old mates (many of whom were fishermen) in a group we christened Fisherman's Friends. Over the years, our Friday nights down by the harbour, singing about ships and storms and sailors and, yes, fish, became a popular tradition in Port Isaac with locals and visitors alike.

Then, quite out of the blue, we were discovered. Subsequent years have been quite an uncharted course for us all. The Fisherman's Friends have performed on the Pyramid stage at Glastonbury, the Albert Hall and Festival Hall, at the Queen's Jubilee flotilla, at Twickenham in front of 85,000 people, as well as extensively touring the rest of the UK. We've received a Gold Disc for our first album, and a BBC award for preserving the Best Traditions of Folk Music, there's been a book and a documentary and most recently the release of the hugely popular feel-good movie, Fisherman's Friends!

But there's no film or song that could capture the joy that I get from my family. Caroline, now a Cornish artist of renown, captures beautiful images of fish and shells and seaweeds and sea life on canvas, while Jake takes all things nautical to inspire his striking designs for his business and surfs the wild North Cornish waves. Theo works as an offshore geologist around our coast to bring about the construction of wind turbines and alternative energies, while George has his own ever-growing fish merchant and provides me with the best of Cornish fish.

SPANISH-STYLE BAKED HAKE

A firm, meaty white fish like hake paired with smoky chorizo and smooth butter beans is a tried and tested combination that always tastes delicious. This easy dinner feels like a real treat on a weeknight for the whole family to enjoy. — Jon Cleave

1 tbsp olive oil

1 large onion, chopped

100g chorizo, sliced

3 cloves of garlic, crushed

1 tsp paprika

250ml white wine

400g tinned chopped tomatoes

400g tinned butter beans

Handful of black olives, sliced

2-4 x 180-200g hake steaks

1 sprig of fresh parsley

1 lemon

Heat the olive oil in a casserole dish, then add the chopped onion and sliced chorizo. Cook gently until the pan is nice and sticky and the onion has reddened.

Add the crushed garlic and after a couple of minutes stir in the paprika. Pour in the white wine, tinned tomatoes, butter beans and sliced black olives. Give everything a good stir, then let it bubble away for 10 minutes or so on a medium heat.

Place the hake steaks on top of the chorizo, tomatoes and beans. Put the lid on the casserole dish, then transfer it to the oven and bake for 12 to 15 minutes at 180°c.

When the hake is done, top the dish with fresh parsley and serve with wedges of lemon for squeezing over the top.

PREPARATION TIME: 5 MINUTES | COOKING TIME: APPROX. 40 MINUTES | SERVES 4

FLYING FISH SEAFOODS

BY JOHNNY GODDEN

"Sourcing from local fishermen is vital in supporting the community and future generations. The knowledge and wisdom we can all learn from speaking with them is essential to not only supplying top-quality produce, but also gaining a real insight into their skillset, history and tales."

I always enjoyed childhood fishing trips on the west coast of Scotland. By the age of 16, I was collecting, cleaning and selling cuttlefish to pet shops for spare change. Upon leaving school my brother, Sandy, found me a job cleaning boxes at the local fish merchants. Here, I learnt the importance of quality and the dedication required to achieve excellence. At 26, I had my own ideas on how a business should be run. Moving to Cornwall was the key to being closer to the source of some of the most beautiful produce, and Flying Fish Seafoods was born.

For the past 14 years our buyers have been up before sunrise to pick the best catch from the day-boats from Brixham, Newlyn and Plymouth markets. From day-netted turbots to handline mackerel, sourcing from local fishermen is vital in supporting the community and future generations. The knowledge and wisdom we can all learn from speaking with them is essential to not only supplying top-quality produce, but also gaining a real insight into their skillset, history and tales. For example, barely a century ago any monkfish caught in fishing nets would be discarded because their appearance made them look like monsters that brought bad luck. Now, these fish sit prime on any restaurant's menu.

The fishing industry is something that is very close to all of our hearts; the vast majority of all the staff at Flying Fish Seafoods have some connection to the fishing or restaurant trade. This love of seafood motivates us to strive for the quality and excellence that our customers have grown to expect. These beliefs and morals fill us with pride and the fact that our produce will be featured on the tables of some of the UK's leading restaurants only exaggerates this.

There are many challenges to our industry, and over the years many curve balls have certainly been thrown our way. One bank holiday Friday I had a phone call at 2am informing me that one of our drivers had been in an accident in London. I jumped in a van and drove straight up to meet him, transferred the fish and continued on. Once completed, I headed home around 12 noon, but en route my heavily pregnant wife Ana phoned me to announce that she had gone into labour! Welcome to the world Coco... That was a very long 37-hour shift!

Photos © Cristian Barnett

BBQ MACKEREL WITH SEA LETTUCE

Catching mackerel and barbecuing on the beach with family, friends and a good bottle of wine is one of those little joys in life that holds so many memories. This recipe was developed out of necessity when cooking tools were limited and nature came up with the answer! – Nick Mason

4 line caught mackerel (I normally catch mine on my kayak)

100g foraged sea lettuce (this can be found on the beach)

Cornish sea salt

1 lemon

4 seeded bread rolls

Salted butter

Start by gutting and cleaning the mackerel; you can always ask your fishmonger to do this for you. Get a barbecue nice and hot.

Lay the sea lettuce in sheets on a plate and place the prepared mackerel on top. Sprinkle with a small amount of Cornish sea salt and wrap the lettuce around each fish individually.

Cut the lemon in half and place both halves flat side down on top of your barbecue, then don't touch them until you need it. You want to generously caramelise the lemon to intensify the flavour.

Place the mackerel parcels on the preheated barbecue and cook for roughly 4 minutes on each side. Don't worry if the heat from the barbecue seems fierce, as the moisture in the sea lettuce helps to protect the fish while adding an intense depth of flavour.

While the parcels are cooking, generously butter the bread rolls.

Gently peel back the sea lettuce to reveal the mackerel and carefully remove the flesh from the bone. Place the charred lettuce and the soft mackerel inside the buttered rolls and finish with a generous squeeze of caramelised lemon juice.

Serve with a very simple leafy or Greek-style salad, and an ice-cold bottle of your favourite plonk!

PREPARATION TIME: 10 MINUTES | COOKING TIME: 10 MINUTES | SERVES 4

FRESH FROM THE BOAT

BY CHANTELLE WILLIAMS

"It's not easy working in the fish industry and it's full of difficult times, long hours and political battles, many of which I didn't know would even exist. But it is the most rewarding industry, and one of the largest families which I am proud to be part of."

I work with my husband Peter Williams, a Hampshire and Sussex based inshore fisherman, and am 100% proud of what we both do. For many years, I worked in an office but then decided to take a leap into the great ocean a few years ago, by supporting my husband in what he does and running my own business buying and selling local fish and shellfish. When Fresh From The Boat was born, I had goals and a vision, but nothing could have prepared me for our achievements so far.

Our whole business ethos is to sell local, seasonal and sustainable fish to local people. The majority of our catch comes from our own boats (Carly D and Tia Maria) or other local inshore sustainable day boats. In this way, food mileage is kept to a minimum and our fish is always super fresh. We catch a wide variety of fish and shellfish in the Solent and even fish for Emsworth oysters at the right time of year.

Fresh From The Boat started by supplying a few local businesses with our fish and shellfish. The list of people who stock them is now huge! I sell our fish to organic farm shops, local fishmongers, restaurants, fish box schemes, and our very own shop, which opened in June 2020. In the same year, we were overwhelmed to receive one of the highest accreditations in the fishing industry from the Master Fishmonger Awards for our mobile fish shop.

I have been involved in many community events including the building of a lobster pot Christmas tree, a Seafood Lunch on Emsworth Quay, and even creating an award-winning film. We have attended the Queen's Patron's Lunch with The Fishermen's Mission, and worked closely with Seafish for the 'Love Your Seafood' campaign. I am also a trustee for Fishing Into The Future, a UK-wide charity acting for sustainable and prosperous UK fisheries.

Most importantly, we are part of an amazing community who support us through the highs and lows of running a fishing boat and a fish business. It's not easy working in the fish industry and it's full of difficult times, long hours and political battles, many of which I didn't know would even exist. But it is the most rewarding industry, and one of the largest families which I am proud to be part of.

GINGER AND LIME DOVER SOLE
WITH SAMPHIRE

· ·

Dover sole is a flatfish with firm flesh that has a delicate, mild and sweet flavour. If you can, ask a fishmonger to prepare it for you. The zingy sauce provides great contrast for an exciting meal that will really wake up your taste buds!
— Chantelle Williams

4 tbsp plain flour

½ tsp chilli powder

Sea salt

Freshly ground black pepper

2 Dover sole, scaled, cleaned, trimmed and dark skin removed (if you can, ask your fishmonger to do this for you)

2 tbsp olive oil

2 red chillies, finely sliced

2 cloves of garlic, finely sliced

300g samphire

140g unsalted butter

50g fresh root ginger, chopped

4 tbsp lime juice (about 3 limes)

2 tbsp chopped fresh coriander

Preheat the oven to 200°c. Combine the flour and chilli powder with some salt and pepper in a bowl, then dust the Dover sole with this mixture, gently shaking off any excess.

Heat a large, non-stick, ovenproof frying pan over a medium-high heat. Add the olive oil, then when it's hot lay the sole into the pan (white skin side down if you've part-skinned them) and fry, without moving them, for 3 to 4 minutes, or until the coating forms a golden-brown crust.

Turn the fish over and transfer the frying pan to the top of the hot oven (or transfer the fish to a warmed baking tray and place in the oven) and cook for a further 8 to 10 minutes, or until the sole are cooked through and the flesh is opaque.

Meanwhile, heat another frying pan with a small amount of olive oil in. Add the sliced red chillies and garlic, then once they are sizzling add the samphire. Pan fry for about 2 to 3 minutes.

To make the sauce, melt the butter in another frying pan over a medium heat, and let it bubble for 2 to 3 minutes, or until it turns a nut-brown colour. Reduce the heat to low, then add the ginger, lime juice and chopped coriander. Warm everything through but don't overheat the sauce or it will separate. Season to taste.

Serve the sole with the samphire and spoon the ginger and lime sauce over the top. It could also be accompanied by new potatoes, chips or jacket potatoes.

JANE DEVONSHIRE

"It's so important to maintain the stocks for future generations and ensure that we're doing our best to support the people making that happen. Little things do have a big impact, so our responsibility as consumers is to be aware of all food's provenance."

I'm particularly passionate about eating British seafood because in my opinion, it's some of the best in the world. There's sometimes a kind of mystique about fish; people think it's difficult to cook but it's really not. Even kids can get involved, making it an accessible and family-friendly ingredient. I wish more people would cook with fresh fish, and if that means stretchy cheese occasionally for those who would not usually eat fish, like in the recipe I've shared for this book, then so be it!

Half of my family on my dad's side were fishermen in Dorset, so there's always been a strong affiliation with the sea and its produce for me. We used to holiday by the sea; my aunty had a big hotel where I'd watch the freshly caught fish being brought into the kitchen and cooked for that night's menu. At home, every Friday was fish, every Sunday we'd have a shellfish supper, and my mum even used to make jellied eels. When I was a contestant on MasterChef in 2016, my starter for the final was based around that shellfish supper and that was part of the reason I won, so it's very special to me.

Today, I invariably cook fish at the end of a long day because it's so quick, and if you're not sure how to prepare something, the internet is always there for answers: I taught myself to fillet a flatfish for MasterChef using video tutorials! Another great way to learn about seafood is to shop at your local fishmongers, because you can ask what they're catching a lot of, or what's harder to get at certain times, and begin to understand the consequences of what you're buying. Even when you go to supermarkets, look for the MSC logo and make sure things like tuna are line-caught and dolphin-friendly.

I try very hard to make sure we only buy and eat sustainable fish, including lots of mackerel for example, because it's so important to maintain the stocks for future generations and ensure that we're doing our best to support the people making that happen. Little things do have a big impact, so our responsibility as consumers is to be aware of all food's provenance. When we do this, we can help to keep prices fair on both sides and enjoy British seafood long into the future.

CHEESY SMOKED HADDOCK FISH FINGERS

· ·

These fish fingers are a fabulous meal and great fun to make. I love to eat them with some very fresh poached eggs, but in the past my kids enjoyed them with baked beans. Alternatively, they can be served with salad or peas. – Jane Devonshire

450g smoked haddock (I use the undyed version)

300ml milk

250g mashed potato

150g broccoli, cooked and chopped (use the stalks as well)

150g frozen peas, cooked

100g strong cheddar, grated

100g pre-grated mozzarella (from a packet)

1 large egg

Black pepper

100g flour

3 eggs, beaten

100g panko breadcrumbs

When I know I am making these, I always cook extra potatoes the night before and keep them for the next day to make this an even quicker meal. It's also one of the few times I buy the pre-grated packaged mozzarella as the whole ones are just too wet and don't work in this recipe. Like all my recipes, this can easily be made gluten-free by using gluten-free breadcrumbs.

Place the smoked haddock in a wide pan on a low heat and cover with the milk. Gently poach the fish until flaky and easily pierced with a toothpick. Remove it from the milk, if necessary peel off the skin and check for bones. Gently flake the fish into a large bowl.

Add the mashed potato, broccoli, peas, cheddar, mozzarella, egg and some black pepper to the bowl with the haddock. Gently combine everything; I find this is easier to do using your hands (or the kids can do it) but try not to break up the fish flakes too much.

Take a sausage-sized piece of the mixture and shape into a fish finger but about twice the usual thickness. Place onto a plate and repeat with all the mixture. You should get between 10 and 12 good portions. The children have always made them this shape in our house, but if you want to make them into fish cakes, please do.

Place the fish fingers in the fridge to chill, preferably for at least 30 minutes although if they are handled carefully you can do the next bit straight away.

Prepare three shallow bowls, one with the flour, one with the beaten eggs, and one with the panko breadcrumbs. Take one of the fish fingers and roll in the flour, then dip into the egg and lastly coat in the breadcrumbs. Place on an oiled baking tray and repeat with the remaining fish fingers. This is a messy process and the kids love it!

Once all the fish fingers are breadcrumbed, drizzle them with oil and then place the tray in a preheated oven at 220°c/200°c fan/Gas Mark 6 to bake for 20 minutes until golden brown. Alternatively, shallow fry the fish fingers in a little oil until golden brown on all sides. Serve straight away.

JCS FISH

BY LOUISE COULBECK

"We're passionate about salmon but believe it must be produced responsibly. So we buy directly from growers we know personally (mainly in Scotland) and have achieved all the key sustainability accreditations."

My husband Andy and I started our family business, JCS Fish, back in 2000 so it's just celebrated its 20th anniversary. We're both from Grimsby families with fishing backgrounds and Andy had spent the first part of his career working for his family firm. But we wanted a new challenge, and Andy had so much knowledge and experience in salmon that a new venture focused on that one fish seemed a natural step. We named it JCS in honour of Jack Carlisle Smith, a local hero in the fish industry who had been an important mentor to Andy in the early part of his career.

Our idea was to make salmon more accessible for everyone. Good quality farmed Atlantic salmon is readily available all year round, so versatile and rich in Omega-3; a perfect fit for anyone who wants to eat more healthily. In 2009 we launched our BigFish retail brand. Our first products were prepared fillets that you can use straight from the freezer, both plain salmon and with interesting marinades like Garden Mint and Thai Spice. We've always been big fans of the freezer; it's such a great way to keep a rich store cupboard on hand and cut down food waste.

A couple of years ago we also built our own smokehouse and introduced BigFish Smoked. We're particularly proud of all the awards we've won: 15 or more just in the last two years, and ten of those for our smoked products, including Great Taste stars and the UK's Best Smoked Fish in the prestigious Quality Food & Drink Awards 2019.

We're passionate about salmon but believe it must be produced responsibly. So we buy directly from growers we know personally (mainly in Scotland) and have achieved all the key sustainability accreditations. We're a 'Chain of Custody' supplier under the Aquaculture Stewardship Council and GlobalG.A.P. schemes, two of the most important for farmed fish. All BigFish Atlantic salmon is now certified either with the GGN (GlobalG.A.P.) label or organic, which has the highest sustainability standards of any kind of farmed fish you can buy. You can also check the sources of all our fish through the Ocean Disclosure Project website.

We're proud of what we've achieved in the last two decades, and with our son Jack and his fiancée, Rosie, having joined the business, we're sure our family enterprise has an exciting future ahead!

SPICED SALMON EN CROUTE

The Romans enjoyed serving fish with spices and sweet fruits, which sounds odd but works surprisingly well with salmon. This richly flavoured dish takes a little preparation, but is perfect for a special occasion, even an alternative Sunday lunch! Any leftovers are delicious served cold the next day. — Louise Coulbeck

35g butter, softened

55g dates, stoned and chopped

5 whole cloves, crushed

1 tbsp raisins

1 tbsp honey

½ tsp Dijon mustard (optional)

¼ tsp ground ginger

¼ tsp ground cumin

Handful of fresh mint, finely chopped

320g pack of ready-made puff pastry

4 BigFish™ salmon fillets, defrosted

Black pepper

A little milk, for glazing

Hollandaise sauce, to serve (ready-made is fine)

Preheat the oven to 220°c/200°c fan/Gas Mark 7. Put the softened butter into a bowl then mix in the dates, cloves, raisins, honey, mustard, ginger, cumin and mint to make a thick paste.

Roll out the ready-made puff pastry into a long rectangle. Put two of the salmon fillets end to end on the pastry at one end, leaving room to fold the pastry over.

Spoon the spicy date paste on top of the salmon fillets and spread it out to cover them evenly. Season with some pepper and then pop the remaining fillets on top, making a 'sandwich' with the filling in the middle.

Use a pastry brush to spread a little milk around the edge of the pastry, then fold the pastry over and seal well to make your parcel. Cut shapes from any spare pastry to decorate the top as you wish, then brush a little more milk over to glaze.

Put the salmon parcel on a baking tray and cover lightly with foil. Cook in the oven for 30 minutes, taking the foil off for the last 10 minutes so the pastry becomes a lovely golden brown.

Serve in slices, with a selection of fresh steamed green vegetables, new potatoes and a little hollandaise sauce on the side.

Tips: You can make this a day in advance if you wish; just wrap the uncooked salmon parcel in cling film and leave in the fridge, then take it out half an hour before you want to cook so it comes to room temperature. For a larger gathering, you can make a bigger version of this recipe to serve 8 using 1.5kg of fresh salmon (in two large fillets) and doubling the quantities of all the other ingredients. With thanks to cookery writer Anne Williams for the inspiration.

PREPARATION TIME: 25 MINUTES | COOKING TIME: 30 MINUTES | SERVES 4

KAMES FISH FARMING

BY STUART CANNON

"We're proud to remain a family farm, and like my father and grandfather always told me, we have to farm for the future. Fish farming is still such a young industry, with so much to offer. It's exciting, and a big responsibility."

I was a farmer's son in Lincolnshire, and thought I would either take the farm over or do something similar when I grew up. But I was also keen for my own adventure. When I was at agricultural college, an article interested me about the beginnings of fish farming in Denmark. I had always loved eating fish and trout fishing. I got a summer job with a wonderful couple in Dumfries, Graeme and Kirsten Gordon, who were establishing themselves as trout farmers and became mentors to me. Graeme persuaded Stirling University that young trout farmers needed aquacultural courses, and I attended the first ever disease management course there.

Kames Fish Farm was set up in 1972 on the west coast of Scotland, and I completely fell in love with the landscape and community of the place. My future wife visited on a holiday and fell in love with it all too, and joined me when she finished university. The experimenting was enormous fun; it was early days for fish farming in the UK and we had so much to discover. One of the most pioneering things we did was also the simplest; we put trout into freshwater and sea lochs. Everyone said we couldn't do it, they needed the flow of a river to survive. But we learned that if you give the fish space, they create their own flow.

We've farmed many fish over the years and travelled all over the world helping to set up farms. But my passion has always remained with trout, which I think is far too underrated, and we now only farm the steelhead. It's a Pacific salmonid, originally, and migrates naturally to the sea. Swimming in our remote, oceanic lochs against a huge volume of water and fast currents makes it big, athletic and strong, with a firm texture and a wonderful, delicate flavour that is truly exceptional.

We're proud to remain a family farm, and like my father and grandfather always told me, we have to farm for the future. Fish farming is still such a young industry, with so much to offer. It's exciting, and a big responsibility. It understandably gets a lot of scrutiny, but if we can do it right, and keep evolving to do it better, ensuring a high fish welfare standard with minimal impact on the environment, then this wonderful source of healthy protein is the most efficient and low-impact you can get. It tastes pretty great too!

SCOTTISH STEELHEAD TROUT GRAVADLAX

....

This recipe is one from my wife, Shelagh. She's fantastic at all sorts of cooking, but after over 40 years of marriage to a fish farmer, her fish dishes are the envy of Argyll! This one really shows off the beautiful quality and texture of our steelhead trout. – Stuart Cannon

2 Scottish steelhead trout fillets (1kg each)

For the marinade

4 tbsp granulated sugar

3 tbsp coarse sea salt

1 tbsp sunflower oil

1 tsp of your favourite malt whisky

Lots of ground black pepper

3 tbsp chopped fresh dill

For the mustard dill sauce

3 tbsp Dijon mustard

2 tbsp chopped fresh dill

2 tbsp caster sugar

1 tbsp white wine vinegar

1 egg yolk

150ml sunflower oil

Salt and black pepper, to season

This recipe is very quick and easy to prepare but then takes its own time to marinate and produce the most delicious, succulent trout gravadlax.

Mix the marinade ingredients together in a bowl. Put the two trout fillets skin side down on a board. Spread the marinade over each fillet, making sure to cover both completely. Sandwich the fillets together with the skins on the outside. Wrap them tightly in a double layer of foil, and then lay the fillets carefully in a shallow, large dish. Place weights on top of the wrapped fillets; a couple of tins will do. I find it easier to put another large dish on top and then balance the weights on the top of that.

Put the weighted dish in the fridge for at least 48 hours and up to 5 days, turning the fillet parcel over every day. Over this time, the ingredients in the marinade will dissolve together and produce a salty, sweet, sticky liquid which will turn the trout fillets into gorgeous, tasty gravadlax.

For the mustard dill sauce

This sauce complements the gravadlax perfectly. Simply whisk the mustard, dill, sugar, vinegar and egg yolk together in a bowl. Then incorporate the oil, whisking well. It should have the consistency of mayonnaise. Season with salt and pepper. This sauce can be made up to 6 hours ahead, and should be kept in the fridge, tightly covered with cling film.

To serve

Unwrap the fillet parcel, and discard the remaining marinade. If you wish, freeze the fillets for 1 hour to firm up the fish, then cut slices – a little thicker than you would for smoked salmon – at an angle to the skin. Serve the trout gravadlax with the mustard dill sauce on the side, some crusty bread rolls or crackers (we recommend Peter's Yard Original Sourdough Crispbreads) and a glass of your favourite malt whisky.

This dish also freezes extremely well, with each marinated fillet wrapped separately in cling film, for up to 2 months. Perfect if you are preparing in advance for Christmas or a celebration.

PREPARATION TIME: 15 MINUTES, PLUS AT LEAST 48 HOURS MARINATING | SERVES A CROWD AT A PARTY

KEENAN SEAFOOD

BY ROBERT SHANKS

"Our mission is to provide our customers with the highest standard of service and a wide range of seafood in a sustainable manner. That's why we have a policy of trying to source as much fish as possible from the local community, to make sure we help our neighbours first."

The Keenan family name has been associated with the fish business for three generations. T Keenan and Sons Fish Merchants was established in 1942 and now trades under the name Keenan Seafood. The company is led by our managing director, Gerry Keenan, whose father and grandfather established the original business. Our Belfast-based company specialises in supplying a full range of fresh and frozen seafood to our many customers, including hotels, restaurants, cafés and fish and chip shops as well as contract caterers, schools and Health Board units throughout Northern Ireland. We also produce a range of convenience fish products for supermarkets and independent retailers.

Fresh fish is sourced each morning from the local ports of Kilkeel, Ardglass and Portavogie as well as from the rest of Scotland and the west of Ireland. Only the finest quality seafood is selected and transported to our premises for further processing and order assembly. Our mission is to provide our customers with the highest standard of service and a wide range of seafood in a sustainable manner. That's why we have a policy of trying to source as much fish as possible from the local community, to make sure we help our neighbours first. We buy about 15 tonnes of fish every week, and have our own team of expert fish filleters who prepare the fish each day to meet customer specifications. Alongside this, we have our own smoking operation to produce popular brands of natural smoked cod, haddock and coley.

Much of the company's recent growth has been through product development. Products such as our Irish Whiskey and Maple Cured Salmon and Traditional Natural Smoked Haddock have been successful in the Great Taste Awards. We also sell a freshly battered cod fillet produced daily by the award-winning Darren Raffo fish and chip shop, and this has proved hugely successful. We are also lucky to have a very energetic, dedicated and committed team in the business who are central to driving the company forward. As people have become more aware of their health, and the benefits of eating fish have become more apparent, Keenan Seafood is well geared to take advantage of the opportunities in this important industry.

MACKEREL, BEETROOT, DASHI AND BACON BROTH, DILL OIL

....

This is a great dish for entertaining if you like to spend time cooking at the weekends. The strong flavour of the brined and poached mackerel against savoury broth, sweet roasted beetroot and fresh herbs is a fantastic contrast and sure to impress your guests.
— Alex Greene, head chef at Deanes Eipic.

For the mackerel

5g seawater powder

30g salt

10g sugar

4 fresh mackerel fillets

Olive oil

For the dashi and bacon broth

500g smoked bacon

30g kombu (edible kelp)

1 carrot

1 red chilli

2 onions

5 celery sticks

12 dried shiitake mushrooms

30g bonito flakes

100ml soy sauce

20ml lime juice

For the beetroot

2kg mixed beetroot (I use Mooncoin)

200g rye flour

70g rock salt

For the dill oil

375g fresh dill

200ml neutral cooking oil

To serve

Sea herbs (aster, purslane and arrow grass work well)

For the mackerel

Put the seawater powder, salt and sugar in a pan with 300ml of water. Bring to the boil and then cool the brine rapidly by pouring it into a jug sitting in a bowl of ice.

Remove the fine membranes and pin-bones from the mackerel, then trim the fillets to your preferred portion size. Put the prepared mackerel into the cooled brine and leave for 30 minutes. After this time, wash off the brine, pat the fish dry and place it in a sealed, airtight, heatproof bag (ideally vacuum packed) with a little olive oil. Poach the brined mackerel at 52°c for 8 to 10 minutes.

For the dashi and bacon broth

Dice the smoked bacon and put it into a large pan with the rest of the ingredients and 3 litres of water. Bring to the boil and simmer for 30 minutes, then leave the pan off the heat for a further 30 minutes for the broth to infuse.

For the beetroot

Wash the beetroot thoroughly then set aside. Combine the flour and rock salt with just enough water to make a pliable dough. Beat the mixture for 5 minutes, then wrap the salt dough around the beetroot individually. Bake the encased beetroot in the oven at 170°c for 20 to 30 minutes until the centre is soft.

For the dill oil

Pick all tops off the dill and place them in a pan with the oil. Bring the temperature of the oil up to 60°c then strain the infused oil through a piece of muslin cloth into a bowl or jug.

To serve

Briefly 'shock' the sea herbs in hot water to bring out their flavour. Carve up the salt-baked beetroot and place it on the plates with the poached mackerel. Pour some of the dashi and bacon broth around the main elements, then drizzle over some of the dill oil. Garnish the dish with the sea herbs and serve.

LISA WILLIAMS
THE ROYAL NAVY

"British seafood is one of a kind and has been a liberating experience for me so far. I have no doubt there are more great things ahead, but I look forward to trying new types of seafood and learning more about the spectacular flavours the sea has to offer."

Coming from the Caribbean, cooking for me is second nature. I cook almost daily and thought: why not do it as a career? The Royal Navy provides the ingredients - sometimes we get what is needed and sometimes we don't - and this is what makes what I do so interesting; I get to put my creativity to the test! Sometimes I produce dishes which turn out to be spectacular, which I'm proud to stand behind and say "I made that"… and sometimes I make mistakes that I learn from.

But in anything that I do, I do it to the best of my abilities. This has earned me a lot more recognition, but it's also made my job challenging; everyone expects me to always produce excellent dishes. It's motivated me to always go the extra mile. I consider myself to be a very lucky individual because so far I've been achieving my goals and I have an excellent support system, including my close friends and family. I know without them I wouldn't be where I am today. On days when I'm at my lowest they push me to look past the trials and aim for excellence.

Being in the Royal Navy has allowed me to learn about so many different places, people and opportunities. But nothing so far has surpassed the British seafood experiences. Since becoming a chef in the Royal Navy I've seen many different ways of preparing seafood. I enjoy preparing seafood, particularly because it's a completely different procedure and needs more love and attention put into creating the final product, making it something to be proud of. I enjoy experimenting and not following a recipe.

If you love eating seafood, learn the different varieties, their unique textures and tastes and just keep adding some of your favourite ingredients to create a dish that you can call yours. Seafood is very delicate which makes it easier to make a mistake and ruin the dish. Turn your mistakes into a lesson. It's easier to take criticism and make decisions to then turn your project into a masterpiece!

British seafood is one of a kind and has been a liberating experience for me so far. I have no doubt there are more great things ahead, but I look forward to trying new types of seafood and learning more about the spectacular flavours the sea has to offer.

DE LI-KINGKLIP

The type of fish I used to create this dish is called Kingklip, a species of cusk eel. Any fish can be used in replacement though; just keep in mind the cooking time will differ depending on the size and type of fish used. The seasoning can be adjusted to personal preference, but this is how I like it. — Lisa Williams

½ lemon

1 kingklip fillet, halved

15g ginger, finely chopped

3 cloves of garlic, finely chopped

2 tbsp olive oil

4 tbsp flour

2 tsp salt

2 tsp lemon and dill fish seasoning

2 tsp ground cumin

2 tsp Chinese five spice

2 tsp garam masala

1 tsp black pepper

1 tsp mild curry powder

1 tsp paprika

500g cooking oil

For the coconut sauce

55g butter

1.1 litres milk

65g flour

1 vegetable stock cube

2½ tbsp sugar

50g desiccated coconut

Begin by squeezing the lemon half over the kingklip fillet. Mix the chopped ginger and garlic with the olive oil and rub the mixture into the fillet. To the flour, add all the remaining ingredients, apart from the cooking oil, and combine thoroughly until they are completely blended together.

Pour the cooking oil into a frying pan and allow it to heat up, but don't let it get to boiling point. Completely coat each half of the kingklip fillet with the seasoned flour and place both pieces into the hot oil. After 5 minutes, flip each piece and cook for a further 5 minutes on the other side before removing from the pan.

For the coconut sauce

Melt the butter in a small pan over a low heat. As the butter is melting, pour the milk into another pan and allow it to come to the boil. Add the flour to the pan with the melted butter, take it off the heat, and completely mix them together. Once they are fully combined the pan can be put back on the heat, allowing the flour to cook. Make sure to keep mixing as it does.

Slowly add a little bit of the boiled milk to the flour and butter paste and keep stirring until it becomes smooth. Do this until all the milk has been added to the mixture. Add the vegetable stock cube and sugar to the mixture, stirring until they have completely melted. Finally, add the desiccated coconut and stir until it is completely integrated to create the sauce.

To serve

Place the fried kingklip on a plate and garnish with the coconut sauce.

PREPARATION TIME: 30 MINUTES | COOKING TIME: 20 MINUTES | SERVES 2

THE MAGPIE CAFÉ

BY IAN ROBSON

"One day a fisherman who had been a school friend of mine came to the kitchen door with a sack full of fresh king scallops and asked if there was anything we could do with them... Since then, local fish and seafood have formed the backbone of our menu and we work closely with nearby suppliers to enable us to serve the finest fresh fish, crabs, lobsters and more."

It is now nearly 50 years since I walked through the kitchen door of The Magpie Café as a lanky teenager, little suspecting the rollercoaster ride I was in for. In the early years I would just help out at weekends and on my two weeks annual holiday from my other full-time job. In the 1970s The Magpie was a seasonal seaside café open from Good Friday, whenever that fell, until the last Sunday in September. My part-time stints in The Magpie led to it 'getting in my blood' and before the end of the decade I had quit my job and committed to a total career change.

One day a fisherman who had been a school friend of mine came to the kitchen door with a sack full of fresh king scallops and asked if there was anything we could do with them. This was the start of The Magpie's transformation into the year-round destination it is today. Since then, local fish and seafood have formed the backbone of our menu and we work closely with nearby suppliers to enable us to serve the finest fresh fish, crabs, lobsters and more. We are particularly lucky to have an excellent working relationship with Whitby's own Lockers Trawlers who, like us, are committed to fresh fish landed into British ports.

The Magpie has always been a family-run business. Way back in the 1950s it was owned by the grandparents, then the parents of my business partner, Alison Slater, and we still have several generations of customers and staff here. Alison and I currently own the business, aided and abetted by head chef Paul Gildroy and restaurant manager Duncan Robson, plus the family members involved in the day to day running of the restaurant, takeaway and our fishmongers, The Whitby Catch, which we added to the business around 10 years ago.

Situated around 100 yards from the restaurant at the other end of the fish market, The Whitby Catch is ideally placed to sell locally landed crabs and lobsters as well as oven-ready meals from the chefs in The Magpie's kitchen. Our fishmongers also have a good online trade via the website selling Whitby fish, seafood and locally smoked kippers all over England, Wales and the Scottish Lowlands by next day courier.

Photos © Tim Green

WHITBY KIPPER 'YORKSHIRE EGGS' WITH PICKLED CUCUMBER AND RHUBARB RELISH

Whitby has long been renowned for the quality of its kippers, and this recipe provides a delicious seaside take on the traditional scotch egg. – Paul Gildroy

For the pickled cucumber

1 cucumber, thinly sliced

1 medium onion, finely sliced

2 tbsp salt

200ml white wine vinegar

2 tbsp caster sugar

1 tsp mustard seeds

4 cloves

For the rhubarb relish

250g sugar

100ml cider vinegar

1 onion, finely chopped

1 thumb-sized piece of fresh ginger, grated

1 tsp salt

½ tsp allspice

500g Yorkshire rhubarb, finely chopped

For the Yorkshire Eggs

6 free-range hen's eggs

400g kipper fillets

75g cream cheese

1 egg yolk

½ lemon, zested

1 tbsp chopped parsley

2 spring onions, very finely sliced

Freshly ground black pepper

Plain flour, for dusting

2-3 eggs, beaten

150g natural breadcrumbs

Oil, for deep frying

75g Wensleydale cheese

For the pickled cucumber

Place the sliced cucumber and onion into a bowl, sprinkle over the salt, mix well, cover and refrigerate for 2 hours. Heat the vinegar, sugar, mustard seeds and cloves until the sugar has dissolved. Rinse the salted cucumber and onion well, then place into a jar and pour over the pickling liquid. Seal the jar with a lid and leave for a minimum of 24 hours before using.

For the rhubarb relish

Place the sugar, vinegar, onion, ginger, salt and allspice into a pan and bring to the boil. Cook until the mixture is syrupy then add the rhubarb. Bring back to the boil, then cook on a low heat for around 30 to 40 minutes, or until the rhubarb has softened and any juices have reduced so the mixture resembles jam. This can be made well in advance and kept in airtight sterilised jars.

For the Yorkshire Eggs

Carefully lower the eggs into a pan of boiling water, then bring back to the boil and cook for 5 minutes. Immediately transfer the eggs to a bowl of iced water to cool.

Meanwhile, put the kipper fillets, cream cheese, egg yolk and lemon zest into a food processor. Blitz until very smooth then stir through the parsley, spring onion and black pepper to taste. Transfer the mixture into a bowl and refrigerate for at least 30 minutes.

Carefully peel the soft-boiled eggs, then roll them in the flour and shake off any excess. Divide the chilled kipper mixture into six portions, then, working one at a time, gently mould it around the eggs. Place the Yorkshire Eggs back into the fridge to firm up. Put some more flour into a shallow bowl, the beaten egg in another and the breadcrumbs in a third.

Roll the Yorkshire Eggs in the flour, gently knocking off any excess, then dip them in the beaten egg, and finally coat them in the breadcrumbs. Heat some oil in a deep pan to 175°c and carefully lower each egg into the oil. Deep fry until golden in colour, about 5 to 6 minutes, then transfer them from the pan onto some kitchen paper to drain.

To serve

Place a few salad leaves and some pickled cucumber in the centre of each plate. Cut each Yorkshire Egg in half and sit the halves on the leaves, then crumble over the Wensleydale cheese and serve with a good spoonful of Yorkshire rhubarb relish on the side.

PREPARATION TIME: APPROX. 30 MINUTES, PLUS 24 HOURS PICKLING | COOKING TIME: APPROX. 1 HOUR | SERVES 6

MARINE
STEWARDSHIP COUNCIL

BY LOREN HILLER

"We all need healthy oceans, so we must act to keep them teeming with life, now and into the future! The oceans define us."

Our oceans cover 70% of our planet. They are vast and furious, beautiful and endlessly fascinating. Unfortunately, these same oceans are under immense pressure. And at a time when a growing global population needs sustainable, low-carbon protein more than ever, a third of fish stocks are overexploited, and the ocean faces unprecedented threats, from global warming to ocean acidification and plastic pollution.

Seafood is our last truly wild major food source, so the stakes are high when we really think about how important it is to protect this resource. But addressing these challenges doesn't mean we have to stop eating fish, nor is it a feasible solution for everyone. Globally, over one billion people rely on fish as their primary source of protein, largely in developing countries.

We all need healthy oceans, so we must act to keep them teeming with life, now and into the future! The oceans define us. They regulate our climate and supply much of the oxygen we need to survive. The life within our oceans is also essential to sustain people's livelihoods, providing incomes for millions around the world. We are all connected in one way or another and we are, at this moment in time, in reach of a whole new relationship with the ocean: a wiser, more sustainable one.

As we have grown more aware of these threats, so has the willingness to work together to find global solutions. One way that you can make a positive change is by choosing the Marine Stewardship Council (MSC) blue label when buying fish and seafood. Choosing fish and seafood with the blue MSC label makes it easier to identify products that have been sourced sustainably from a well-managed fishery with limited impacts on the environment. The MSC's approach means that everyone can play a part in safeguarding the future of our oceans and seafood supplies. When you buy a product with the blue fish label, you become part of a virtuous circle, helping to protect the productivity and health of our oceans. The collectiveness of humanity can return our oceans to their glory, so that they remain ecologically abundant and capable of feeding the world. So, next time you are out shopping or in a restaurant, #choosethebluefish, and let's ensure there is plenty of fish and seafood for future generations.

© If Berglund

© Fish City

© Emma Rance

© Emma Rance

CERTIFIED
SUSTAINABLE
SEAFOOD
MSC
www.msc.org

© Emma Rance

sh City

CLAM AND CHORIZO PASTA
WITH PARSLEY GREMOLATA

I love cooking with clams! They are easy to prepare, really meaty and delicious in pasta! The clams used in this recipe are sourced from the small scale Poole Harbour Clam & Cockle Fishery, which is MSC certified as a sustainable and well managed fishery. — Loren Hiller

For the clam and chorizo pasta

24 MSC certified Poole Harbour clams (or other MSC clams, just look for the blue label)

½ white onion

2 cloves of garlic

100g spicy chorizo sausage (not cooking chorizo)

160g dried spaghetti

2 handfuls of cherry tomatoes, halved

200ml dry white wine

Pinch of salt and pepper

For the parsley gremolata

Handful of fresh flat leaf parsley

1 clove of garlic, grated

1 lemon, zested

For the clam and chorizo pasta

Before cooking, check for any broken shells or clams that don't close when tapped; these are dead and shouldn't be eaten. Any dirty shells need to be scrubbed clean. Finely dice the onion and garlic, and dice the chorizo. Place all three ingredients in a pan over a medium heat and season with salt. You shouldn't need any oil as the chorizo will naturally release its own oils. Stirring frequently, cook until the onion and garlic are tender, usually around 10 to 12 minutes.

Bring a pan of water to the boil for your spaghetti. Salt the water and cook the spaghetti until al dente, or 1 minute before the final cooking time recommended on the packaging.

Once the onions are tender, add the tomatoes and let them soften slightly. Pour in the wine and allow to bubble and reduce. Now for the fun part! Place your clams into the pan, put the lid on and allow them to steam. When the clams are cooked they'll pop open. This should take 3 to 5 minutes (any clams which do not open should be discarded).

Take the spaghetti out with tongs, reserving the cooking water, and place the pasta into the pan of clams. Stir to incorporate all of the ingredients. Put a tablespoon of the pasta water into the pan with the other ingredients. Season with salt and pepper to taste.

For the parsley gremolata

Finely chop the parsley until it's almost minced (don't use a food processor). Stir the garlic and lemon zest into the parsley and chop a little more to get everything incorporated.

To serve

Serve the clam and chorizo pasta in bowls and sprinkle over the parsley gremolata. Enjoy!

PREPARATION TIME: 10 MINUTES | COOKING TIME: 20 MINUTES | SERVES 2

MARK MCGORRIN

"The chef offers a great choice and the crew often go for meat, but for me it's fish every day... Doing 12 hour shifts, 7 days a week, I do work up a big appetite. When I step off Kirkella after a long trip, I feel fit and healthy."

Growing up in Peterhead, everyone's family were either into fishing, farming or the oil industry. For me, fishing was the natural choice and I started off very young, at the age of 16, on the PD220 Aquila where I stayed for many years, gaining experience and studying for my Class 2 fishing ticket. This led me to the Arctic Warrior as an officer on deck and with further study, I gained my Class 1 ticket, giving me the opportunity to join Kirkella, the biggest white fish trawler in the UK, as the chief mate.

I've since worked with UK Fisheries to create a great relationship with Peterhead's Maritime College, and many trainees join the Kirkella and other company vessels. One of my best memories, and proudest moments, was sailing the Kirkella up the Thames and under Tower Bridge, where the Princess Royal christened the boat.

The Kirkella, based in Hull, is part of the distant waters fleet travelling many miles to catch cod. We supply approximately 8% of all fish served by UK fish and chip shops. The only problem is that it's 1,500 miles away and it takes us 5 days to get there! There are plenty of cod, but we work within strict quotas to ensure sustainable fishing. Cod are demersal, meaning they swim in deep water, and we have to shoot very long lines and nets to catch them. The best are found along the Norwegian coast and Svalbard areas. You can imagine how cold it is in the winter, but we never stop fishing, even in storms and blizzards.

Kirkella is a large factory vessel, meaning fish can be caught, filleted and frozen within 40 minutes of swimming in the sea so it's very fresh and tasty. The chef offers a great choice and the crew often go for meat, but for me it's fish every day. My favourite is just simple breaded fish and chips. Doing 12 hour shifts, 7 days a week, I do work up a big appetite. When I step off Kirkella after a long trip, I feel fit and healthy.

When I'm at home with my partner, Shirley, I love to cook, experimenting and trying new recipes for cod, haddock, sole and monkfish. We live in Peterhead, the busiest fishing port in Britain, so we're never in short supply. When we met, I think our first date was fish and chips!

BAKED COD WITH CHEESE AND CHIVE SAUCE

I love my job. Where else can you sail past stunning Norwegian fjords, take in the Northern Lights and encounter schools of whales for free? And of course, sample the freshest of fish, just out of the sea. I catch the fish; Shirley cooks it. – Mark McGorrin, chief mate, the Kirkella.

4 pieces of fresh cod, skinned and boned

Black pepper

25g unsalted butter

Small bunch of fresh chives, finely chopped

A few sprigs of fresh dill, finely chopped

300ml crème fraîche

150ml milk

150ml double cream

200g cheese, grated

To serve

New potatoes

Baby carrots

Splash of Glayva or Drambuie

Drizzle of honey

Extra sprigs of dill

Preheat the oven to 200°c or 180°c fan. Take the cod out of the fridge, season with black pepper and let it rest on a plate for about 10 minutes while you gather the other ingredients.

Melt the butter in a large frying pan. I prefer to use unsalted butter as the crème fraîche gives this sauce a slight sharpness. When it's nice and hot, add the cod along with a handful of chopped chives and dill. Fry for a few minutes then place the cod into an ovenproof dish and set aside.

To the same pan, add the crème fraîche and milk along with the remaining chopped dill and more chives, keeping some back to garnish the dish. Simmer for a few minutes, then add the cream and most of the cheese. Season to taste. If you love seafood, why not add some prawns to the sauce too.

Pour the sauce over the cod in the ovenproof dish, top with the remaining cheese and bake in the preheated oven for 15 to 20 minutes.

While the cod is baking, prepare your vegetables. Boil the new potatoes until tender, then drain and keep warm in the oven with a knob of butter and some of the chopped chives. Steam or simmer the baby carrots until tender. Now, while a whisky sauce doesn't really go with the fish, it does add a nice touch to glazed carrots. Pour some Glayva or Drambuie into a saucepan and add the honey. Once bubbling, toss in the cooked carrots for a couple of minutes until coated and glazed.

Remove the baked cod from the oven and plate up along with the new potatoes and glazed baby carrots. Sprinkle over the remaining chives and garnish with the extra sprigs of dill. Pour yourself another nip of liqueur and enjoy!

MARK MCGORRIN

PREPARATION TIME: 10 MINUTES | COOKING TIME: 20 MINUTES | SERVES 4

MEL SHAND

"The River Dee in Aberdeenshire flows for 88 miles from the mountains to the sea, and as a Director of the River Dee Trust I have come to know and love it, and the wildlife it supports, very well. The work of the Trust is guided by the principal of how we can better understand and support the river for future generations."

I was brought up by the sea, at Fortrose on the Moray Firth, and have fond memories of trailing my hand in the water behind the boat as porpoises followed. Four years at Art College in Dundee meant the Esks and the coast at St Andrews were visited in almost equal measure, but St Cyrus has pulled my heartstrings since I was a teenager. I had barely dipped a fishing rod in the water when London beckoned but I soon came to my senses, moving back to Deeside in the noughties. I married a fishing ghillie called Hedge and in the best tradition of poacher turned gamekeeper, we came to the Finzean Estate in 2002 where we have raised three boys and far too many dogs. Our lives have turned with the seasons ever since.

Hedge is a landlubber – he famously felt seasick standing on the pier in Oban – so when a stalking client offered to take us mackerel fishing it took Hedge five years to 'fess up' the offer to me. We have fished off Gourdon annually ever since and seen quite a decline in the catch. Whether that is due to not wearing our 'lucky pants' or the steady warming of the water and climate we're not sure. If anything good has come of a worldwide pandemic, it's the knowledge that we can change if we want to.

The River Dee in Aberdeenshire flows for 88 miles from the mountains to the sea, and as a Director of the River Dee Trust I have come to know and love it, and the wildlife it supports, very well. The work of the Trust is guided by the principal of how we can better understand and support the river for future generations. We aim to improve our knowledge and practices to help with practical improvements and restoration of the river as well as delivering information and education across the North East of Scotland.

As an artist and photographer I document the life around me as part of my process. The love for my community inspired a project called A Portrait of Our Time, which led to a Portrait of the River Dee and the creative and educational project called A River of Fish. I've written and directed three community plays; the second won an EPIC award for Scotland for community engagement with the arts. I'm currently writing my third which will revisit A River of Fish. At the end of the day, the river still runs into the sea.

Photos © Mel Shand

SMOKED MACKEREL PÂTÉ

I've made gallons of this, losing any fear of catering for large numbers.
It's completely foolproof and I've never found a better recipe! — Mel Shand

100g butter

350g smoked mackerel fillets

1 lemon, juiced

Salt and pepper, to taste

150ml cream

Gently melt the butter in a pan. Skin the mackerel fillets and whizz them in the food processor (or chop finely by hand) before adding the melted butter, fresh lemon juice and seasoning.

Transfer the mixture from the food processor to a bowl. Softly whip the cream and fold into the mackerel, adding more lemon juice to taste.

Pack the pâté into containers and serve at room temperature with melba toast (for that '80s vibe) or sourdough and sliced tomatoes.

This freezes beautifully and defrosts quickly for emergency lunches. It's also great on oatcakes or seeded crackers and behaves itself in the picnic basket too!

PREPARATION TIME: 10 MINUTES | SERVES 4

MICHAEL WRIGHT

....

"So often I saw a catch being off-loaded from a fishing boat's hold, straight into a huge refrigerated lorry, and whisked away ... it seems that too few of us regularly buy local fish to prepare at home."

Have we, the UK and Ireland, largely lost the skills and desire to enjoy seafood in our homes? My feeling is that the answer is yes, unfortunately. It's embarrassing to admit that, other than when out to dinner, I have rarely eaten locally sourced seafood. The realisation of that failure came sharply into focus during the Covid-19 pandemic. Instead of spending the summer aboard my nine-metre yacht (a Nicholson 31) cruising in British and Irish waters, there has been plenty of time to reflect on the five three-month voyages I have made around these islands since 2012, and to venture into buying local seafood.

From my home port of Falmouth, I have sailed over 7,000 nautical miles and stopped in more than 120 places, many with active fishing fleets and others where fishing has all but ceased. So often I saw a catch being off-loaded from a fishing boat's hold, straight into a huge refrigerated lorry, and whisked away. My quayside conversations and observations have led me to believe that the vast majority of seafood from these waters has been heading to Europe and beyond, such as Cornish crabs being air freighted to China. Other than through restaurants and our omnipresent fish and chip shops, it seems that too few of us regularly buy local fish to prepare at home. When we do buy fish, all too often it is from a supermarket that has 'responsibly sourced' fish from abroad.

One of my personal seafood highlights was at a party where we ate barbecued Cornish mackerel. They had been caught the day before by family members on a pleasure boat out of Mevagissey, cooked by local friends who knew what to do, and were absolutely delicious. More recently, thanks to a conscious desire to support local businesses, my wife and I have enjoyed local crab, lobster, turbot and loads of scallops. I found that preparing my first ever cooked crab was far easier than I had feared, courtesy of YouTube tutorials! I'm now confident that there's a video to guide me through the preparation of any fish or crustacean.

Putting aside debate on the cost of local fish and how to make it more affordable, we should all be encouraged to hone, or learn, the skills we need to enjoy the abundant produce offered by the seas around these islands every day of the year.

FISH FILLETS ON MEDITERRANEAN VEGETABLES

On arriving in port on a small boat, when there is time, I like to get readily available fresh ingredients for a quick, simple, appetising meal, preferably using no more than two pans. When ashore, I use the smaller quantity of pasta, but eat more when I'm sailing. — Michael Wright

2 tbsp olive oil

8 shallots

3 cloves of garlic

I red pepper

I aubergine

I courgette

200-300g pasta

2 x 390g tins or cartons of chopped tomatoes

50g black olives, pitted

I tbsp capers

I tsp sugar

Salt and pepper

4 x 150g fish fillets (haddock or cod are best)

Heat the olive oil in a large frying pan with a lid while you peel and finely chop the shallots and garlic, then add the prepared shallots and garlic to the pan.

Deseed and roughly chop the red pepper then add it to the pan when the shallots and garlic are translucent.

Cut the aubergine and courgette in half lengthways then roughly slice them into crescents. Put them in the pan when the pepper has softened. Cook until the aubergine and courgette are golden, which should take 5 to 10 minutes.

Add the pasta to a large pan of slightly salted boiling water and cook for 13 to 15 minutes.

While the pasta cooks, put the tomatoes, olives, capers and sugar into the frying pan with the vegetables. Bring to the boil then season to taste.

Reduce the heat under the frying pan to a simmer and put the fish fillets on the bed of vegetables. Cover with the lid and cook until the fish is cooked through (approximately 8 to 10 minutes).

Briefly put the fish fillets to one side, drain the cooked pasta and stir it into the Mediterranean vegetables. Replace the fish on top of the pasta and sauce, then serve straight from the pan.

THE NATIONAL LOBSTER HATCHERY

BY CLARE STANLEY

"As someone who loves nothing more than being at sea, fishing, and dining on delicious native seafood, it makes me happy to know I am helping to 'put back' when it comes to our vital but fragile marine resources."

I am the Business Development Manager at the National Lobster Hatchery and I feel incredibly privileged to be playing a role in such an important pioneering project. As someone who loves nothing more than being at sea, fishing, and dining on delicious native seafood, it makes me happy to know I am helping to 'put back' when it comes to our vital but fragile marine resources.

The NLH is a small yet mighty marine conservation charity that aims to help conserve native lobster populations and ultimately protect the long term future of our fishing heritage and all it supports. As well as our education and research outputs, we have a unique and innovative lobster stock enhancement programme. This involves raising baby lobsters at the hatchery until they reach the point where they are better able to survive in the wild. This is when we release them into our native waters, with the help of local fishermen and dive schools.

A female lobster can carry in the region of 4,000 to 40,000 eggs but only one of these eggs is expected to survive in the wild. Our conservation programme helps improve the survival rate dramatically by helping to protect juvenile lobsters during their earliest life stages when they are most vulnerable, especially to predators. Our mission is becoming increasingly important, not just in the UK, but as a model for fisheries and coastal community management worldwide. With more than 75% of global fish stocks either exploited, depleted or recovering, and demand for seafood at an all-time high, we are not only helping to conserve vulnerable lobster populations in the UK, but we are educating the public and future recruits to the industry on the importance of not just a more sustainable fishery but also being sustainable in their everyday lives and consumer choices.

The NLH has received numerous awards for our charitable achievements and innovation. In 2019, we received a Silver Award for Best Wildlife Friendly Attraction and were commended for Best Small Attraction at the Cornwall Tourism Awards. As a global centre of expertise, our work is also recognised internationally and our fun and educational visitor centre in Padstow welcomes over 45,000 visitors each year. We have now released well over a quarter of a million juvenile lobsters into coastal waters, and we are confident this is making a positive impact on the sustainability of Cornwall's lobster fishery and the communities that it supports.

Alex Hyde

© Alex Hyde

Alex Hyde

© Johnny Fenn

Alex Hyde

© Alex Hyde

ASIAN STYLE OVEN-BAKED SEA BASS

This recipe was created by my lovely neighbour Chrissie Taylor and I love it! It also works with other white fish and I'd always opt to use one that is considered sustainable at the time, such as pollock. See www.cornwallgoodseafoodguide.org.uk for advice on which fish are recommended as sustainable. — Clare Stanley

1 whole sea bass (from a sustainable source)

Sea salt

Black pepper

2 cloves of garlic, crushed

3cm fresh ginger, peeled and grated

2 fresh red chillies, diced

2 lemongrass stalks, cut diagonally into small pieces

2 tbsp light soy sauce

1 small tin of coconut cream

Handful of cherry tomatoes

3 spring onions, chopped

Handful of fresh coriander, to taste

Ensure the fish is fully cleaned and gutted with the gills and any threads within removed. I like to keep the head on but you can remove the head if preferred. Slash the flesh on both sides of the fish, if it's not already done, and season it inside and out with salt and black pepper.

Mix together the crushed garlic, grated ginger, diced chilli and lemongrass, plus a pinch of sea salt and black pepper. Finally, add the light soy sauce to the mixture. Let the whole fish marinate in this mixture for at least 30 minutes.

Place the fish, including all the remaining marinade, in a piece of foil and add the coconut cream. Wrap the foil around the fish and crimp the edges to seal it at the top, forming a parcel. Make sure there is still some space around the fish.

Place the foil parcel in the oven and bake for 20 to 30 minutes at 170°c. Halfway through the cooking time, remove the foil parcel from the oven, open it up and add the handful of cherry tomatoes and the chopped spring onions, making sure to close it again before putting it back in the oven for the remaining cooking time. Once fully baked, leave to stand for 5 minutes before opening the foil parcel.

To serve

I like to serve this dish with a few coriander leaves scattered on top and rice on the side, fried lightly with a little butter and light soy sauce, along with some seasonal leafy veg.

PREPARATION TIME: 15 MINUTES, PLUS 30 MINUTES MARINATING | COOKING TIME: 20-30 MINUTES | SERVES 2

A PASSION FOR SEAFOOD

BY MIKE WARNER

"I fervently believe in eating home-grown produce and no more so than when it comes to the wild harvest of our seas. As an island nation, we consume only a fraction of our landings, preferring instead to import the characterless commodities of farmed salmon, tuna, warm water prawns and the like."

I grew up by the sea in coastal Suffolk, which instilled in me a deep love of salt water and everything swimming therein. My first seafood encounter was with my father and a live lobster he'd plucked from the rocks at low tide. I was instantly enthralled, and so began a lifetime of seafood passion: catching, cooking, eating, writing and more recently, selling, almost to the point of obsession.

I'm never happier than when at sea, hauling my few lobster pots or being aboard other fishing vessels. I spend innumerate hours frequenting the haunts of fishermen around the UK coastline; the quays, harbours, slipways, beaches and fish markets are where I feel most at home. The sound of idling diesel engines, the crash of fish boxes, the creaking and crying of gulls and general clatter and hubbub of everyday life at a busy fishing port provide the backdrop to my working life.

As for the seafood? I'm often asked which is my favourite. It's a tough one. I fervently believe in eating home-grown produce and no more so than when it comes to the wild harvest of our seas. As an island nation, we consume only a fraction of our landings, preferring instead to import the characterless commodities of farmed salmon, tuna, warm water prawns and the like. We spurn the diverse, indigenous, seasonal fisheries of our shallow seas and, as the late and very great Keith Floyd once announced, "when it comes to cooking seafood, we've lost our grandparents' nerve."

So what to cook? As an East Coast native, one particular fishery dominated our coastline for generations and is still held by some with such reverence that its moniker 'King of the Sea' is rightly justified. The migratory North Sea herring, a one-time staple for many and now so sadly neglected, would be my seasonal and very affordable choice. Clupea harengus, or 'silver darlings' as they're often known, have intrigued me for years and are a species that I hold with great affection. As with all fish cookery, less is always more, and herring are no exception which is why I've chosen to use them for my recipe in this book.

BAKED AUTUMN HERRING
WITH LEMON AND TOMATO

· ·

I've demonstrated this recipe on many occasions. It looks spectacular, tastes delicious and yet is so simple to make. Best served with fresh sourdough bread and some homemade lemon mayonnaise on the side. – Mike Warner

4 fresh whole longshore herring (with roe, but gutted and cleaned)

1 large lemon, sliced

2 large late season tomatoes, halved

Light olive oil or cold-pressed rapeseed oil

Freshly ground black pepper

Sea salt

Score the herring lightly on each side and pin the tails to the heads using cocktail sticks.

Line a shallow baking tray with foil and grease with a little oil. Place the herring on the foil and lay a slice of lemon on each one.

Add the halved tomatoes to the tray and sprinkle everything liberally with the oil. Finish with good grinding of black pepper and sea salt.

Bake the herring in a preheated oven at 180-200°c for 20 minutes, or until the skin crinkles and parts and the lemon and tomato blacken.

Serve the herring immediately with freshly baked sourdough and homemade lemon mayonnaise.

PREPARATION TIME: 5 MINUTES | COOKING TIME: 20 MINUTES | SERVES 4

PEMBROKESHIRE SCALLOPS

BY NEIL WALTERS

"It is very beautiful; some days you can point the camera in any direction and get a shot worthy of any magazine. Working in the Pembrokeshire Marine National Park is an honour."

We had always wondered why no one had done scallop diving here: cold and bloody hard work is your answer. We are still the only company in Wales who hand-dive for scallops. We had to learn a crazy amount of stuff before we could sell anything. But here we are, nearly six years later!

Just as most of the UK divers are putting their gear away for winter, we are getting ours out. We have a six month winter dive season for scallops here in Wales, bringing you the finest scallops that Wales has to offer. When Mother Nature allows us to, of course! It is very beautiful; some days you can point the camera in any direction and get a shot worthy of any magazine. Working in the Pembrokeshire Marine National Park is an honour.

We have been graced along the way with several awards and have gotten to meet lots of people, even a few famous ones! We've also had an episode about us on the TV, giddy heights for scallop divers from Wales. Being recognised for our hard work has kept us going too; it's always nice to have something else to dust back at HQ!

We have rewritten the book on scallop diver safety and are happy to share it far and wide. One of the protocols we launched was Tee O 3 or 'triangle of orange'. Shellfish divers are a rare breed of commercial divers as they dive alone and are untethered from the boat. This has in the past led to divers in other countries being lost. Our divers wear orange fins and an orange hood. This makes a triangle of orange for the air-sea rescue parties to find them more easily, and we are hoping that other dive crews will follow suit. No one should ever be hurt bringing scallops to the table.

We are always looking to the future and we have decided that as well as scallops, we will soon be farming seaweed. As with any business, sometimes you have to diversify a little. We like our sustainable approach though: farming rather than just taking, only taking what you grow and leaving Mother Nature to do her own thing. As well as growing our own produce in the sea, helping others to do the same is in the future for us as well. We hope that Pembrokeshire will be the place to come for budding AquaNaut sea farmers. Watch this space!

BAKED SCALLOPS WITH
CHEDDAR AND GARLIC MASH

· ·

We wanted alternatives to pan fried scallops. Everyone pan fries, they all do it for different times using different methods but still... frying is frying. This recipe is a little different. Honest, tasty and visually stunning, a marriage of ingredients from the land and sea of Britain's favourite coastal county, Pembrokeshire. — Neil Walters

1 large Maris Piper Pembrokeshire potato, peeled

1 Pembrokeshire King Scallop (Pecten Maximus), shucked and cleaned

Knob of butter

Splash of milk

2-3 cloves of garlic, finely chopped

1-2 spring onions, finely chopped

Pinch of dried seaweed (optional)

1 lemon, juiced

Salt and black pepper, to taste

Cheddar cheese, grated (enough to cover the mash)

This is quite a loose recipe so you can mess around with it, make it yours. Add herbs, spices, different cheeses: this version is just a great start. The mash steams the scallop inside, the flavours all combine and the end result should be crispy cheese, lovely mash and a perfect scallop waiting for you inside.

Preheat the oven to 200°c or 180°c fan. Peel the potato and place in a pan of boiling water. While that is boiling you want to clean and shuck the scallop. If the scallop is fresh, please shuck and then rinse for 10 minutes as per Seafish guidelines. Pat the scallop dry with a paper towel and place on the plate. Make sure to keep the shell as this will be used in the presentation. It needs to be cleaned inside with a nail brush, or equivalent, and then left to dry.

Mash the potato with the knob of butter and splash of milk. Add the garlic and spring onions. If you are adding the seaweed, sprinkle that into the mash at this point. Mix everything together thoroughly until the ingredients are evenly distributed.

Put the clean shell on a tea towel to stabilise it. Place the scallop in the centre of the shell and add the lemon juice, salt and pepper. Pipe on the mash, making sure the scallop is fully covered. Alternatively, you can use a fork to place the mash on the scallop, making sure there are lots of ridges in the potato. The whole thing should look like a mashed potato igloo on the shell. Add a little more salt and pepper. Sprinkle with the cheddar cheese; everyone is different here and I like lots of cheese but don't murder it. Place the scallop shell in the oven for 20 to 25 minutes or until the cheese is nicely brown. The secret here is to watch it. A Yorkshire pudding tray works to hold the shells if you are doing a few. When taking the shells out of the oven be careful as they will be hot.

To serve

Serve with julienned carrots in a butter glaze. Alternatively, a bed of flavoured rice works and it helps support the shell on the plate. Sprinkle on salt and pepper to taste and you are off.

PEMBROKESHIRE SCALLOPS

· ·

PAGE 116

PENGELLY'S FISHMONGERS

BY HAYLEY PHILLIPS

"It can be full on at times, but we really enjoy the buzz when it's busy. We are so passionate about the industry and consistently promote it to get young people involved wherever we can."

Pengelly's Fishmongers is famous for its quality day boat fish and is perfectly situated on the quayside at Looe Harbour. We offer perfect examples of fresh Cornish fish, caught and landed by the day boat fleet of hand liners, netters and trawlers so there's lots of varieties of fish available. Pengelly's was established in 1946 and has been independently owned ever since. Our ethos, on which the business has built its brilliant reputation, is still the same: to supply the very best fish and provide the very best service.

The fishmongers is owned and run by our family; myself and my husband Rob have always had connections with the sea and can't imagine it being any other way. From a young age, Rob learnt the trade as a Saturday boy in his local fishmongers. He now has his own passionate team of staff and Pengelly's continues to thrive and expand. It can be full on at times, but we really enjoy the buzz when it's busy. We are so passionate about the industry and consistently promote it to get young people involved wherever we can. We do this by holding demonstrations in schools or taking on young people to train.

We think there are a few things that make Pengelly's special. Firstly, our location on the quay is perfect for landing fish directly as the boats come in. This gives us the direct opportunity to have the pick of some of the finest species of fish on Cornwall coasts, from the small day boat fleet of Looe and Polperro. Additionally, the port of Looe is tidal so the boats must come and go as quickly as the tide allows, meaning any fish landed here is always under 24 hours old and of exceptional quality. It's handled and stored very little, and as a result the quality is exceptional.

I believe we stand out for the consistency and quality of our products, and over the years Pengelly's has proved it has the ability to adapt to the ever-changing needs of the consumer. We can also deliver to anywhere in mainland UK with next day delivery, so anybody can enjoy the lovely fish that Looe has to offer. We're always pioneering new products to promote our industry and love the work we do.

Looe's Own Day Caught Fish & Shellfish
As seen on BBC's Coast
Pengelly's Fishmongers
Looe 01503 262246. Liskeard 01579 340777

ROAST TURBOT, SAMPHIRE, CUCUMBER, GRAPE AND CLAM BEURRE BLANC

This dish is very simple but has many flavours that tantalise the palate, leaving you wanting the next bite as soon as possible! – Chef Lee Calver

180g turbot fillet (about 5cm thick)

5 palourde clams

100g cucumber

3 seedless black grapes

75g samphire

100g white wine

50g white wine vinegar

100g double cream

2 tbsp vegetable oil

Cornish sea salt, to taste

120g unsalted butter

Place the turbot fillet on some kitchen towel to dry out. Put the clams into a bowl and run under cold water for 5 minutes to remove any dirt and sand. Slice the cucumber in half lengthways. Scrape out the seeds with a spoon then cut the cucumber into thin slices. Cut each grape into 3 slices lengthways and set aside. Rinse the samphire under cold water for 1 minute, then drain thoroughly and leave to dry.

Place a small saucepan on a high heat, and when it starts to smoke pour the cleaned clams and the wine in with care as it will bubble vigorously. Once the clams are open, remove them with a slotted spoon and place to one side. Add the white wine vinegar to the remaining wine in the pan and reduce the liquid by half. Stir in the double cream and gently simmer for a further 5 minutes.

Add the vegetable oil to a non-stick frying pan and place over a medium heat. Season the turbot with the salt and lay the fillet away from you into the hot oil. Leave this to cook for 4 minutes.

Meanwhile, dice 100g of the cold butter, then gradually whisk the cubes into the creamy clam sauce. It should take on a shine and develop a rich buttery flavour. Once all the butter is incorporated, turn the heat down to low, stirring every minute to ensure the sauce doesn't split.

When the turbot has had 4 minutes on one side, gently turn over to the other side. Add the remaining butter to the pan and baste the fish for 1 minute, then remove the turbot from the pan and place it on some clean kitchen towel to rest.

Add the cucumber slices to the beurre blanc (your clam sauce) and remove the saucepan from the heat. Bring some water to the boil in another saucepan and drop the samphire in to cook for 2 minutes. Drain the samphire thoroughly.

Finally, take the clams out of their shells and stir them into the sauce. Give it another taste to check the seasoning, adding salt if required.

To serve

Spoon the clam beurre blanc into the middle of the plate and then place the samphire on top. Sit the turbot on top of the samphire and place the grape slices evenly around the plate. The dish looks so pretty this way, and tastes delicious!

PREPARATION TIME: 20 MINUTES | COOKING TIME: 25-30 MINUTES | SERVES 1

RACHEL GREEN

"As a chef, cooking with fish offers me the flexibility and inspiration to use alternatives. For example, I very often replace cod with haddock or coley, and I will also continue to champion sustainability and neglected species of fish like skate, pollock, herring and gurnard."

Fish has played a very important role in my life, not least because I was born in Grimsby and visiting the docks for fresh fish was part of my childhood. Ever since I can remember, fish has been on the menu, not just in my professional capacity as a chef, but also at home, where we eat fish at least three times a week. It's a healthy option for my family, and I love cooking with it. The key things to remember are not to cook fish on a high heat for too long; handle it carefully as it can be fragile; and it can be rested in a warm place for a few minutes after cooking. Treat it with respect and you'll be rewarded with the most delicious flavours.

Fishing has always fascinated me, and as a chef I was eager to learn more about the different types of fish and how to use them when developing my recipes. When I write a menu which includes fish, I always consult Rob, my fish merchant, as he can immediately advise on what is available and offer me the best quality. The great thing about British seafood is the seasonality, which means there is always something good to look forward to, even though it's affected by the elements as a wild food. Good weather delivers an abundance of fish, and bad weather can create a shortage.

Fish never lets me down though; it's an absolute pleasure to prepare, cook and eat. I always associate a good fish dinner with celebrations, especially Easter. Good Friday meant a whole baked cod with sage and onion stuffing, speck bacon, onion gravy, mushy peas and delicious creamed potatoes. These days I enjoy lighter fish dishes with spices, fresh herbs and coconut. My absolute favourite is a whole roasted fish, cooked in our wood-fired oven with olive oil, lemon, fresh garden herbs and served with aioli. I also have a passion for Grimsby smoked haddock, which produces the most flavoursome kedgeree.

As a chef, cooking with fish offers me the flexibility and inspiration to use alternatives. For example, I very often replace cod with haddock or coley, and I will also continue to champion sustainability and neglected species of fish like skate, pollock, herring and gurnard. I am proud to celebrate Britain's finest fish in this book, and in my work as a Seafish ambassador for this great industry.

SPICED SEAFOOD TAGINE

With flavours from the Middle East, this hearty stew is rich and warming, perfect for a dinner to share. It's fresh, fruity and full of spices. We love the companionship between soft white fish and sweet tomatoes too. — Rachel Green, Seafish ambassador

3 tbsp olive oil

3 cloves of garlic, finely chopped

1 large white onion, thinly sliced

1 tsp cumin seeds

2 tsp ground cumin

2 tbsp paprika

2 tsp ras el hanout

½ tsp cayenne pepper

400g tinned chopped tomatoes

400g tinned chickpeas

100g dried apricots, chopped

1 lemon, zested

1 bay leaf

400ml fish stock

Salt and pepper

500g cod loin (or a mixture of white fish)

6 large raw Mediterranean prawns

Fresh coriander leaves, chopped

To serve

600g couscous, cooked

50ml natural yoghurt

Heat a heavy-based casserole dish on a medium heat. Add the oil, then fry the garlic and onion for a few minutes until softened.

Increase the heat and add the cumin, paprika, ras el hanout and cayenne pepper, then fry for around 1 minute. Reduce the heat.

Add the chopped tomatoes, chickpeas, apricots, lemon zest, bay leaf and fish stock. Season with salt and pepper to taste and simmer for 10 to 15 minutes, stirring regularly.

Cut the cod loin into large pieces and add them to the dish. Ensure that the cod is covered with the sauce to infuse the fish with the spices.

Cover the dish with a lid and reduce the heat to low. Continue to cook for 5 to 8 minutes until the fish is cooked through. If the tagine looks too thick, add a little more stock.

Meanwhile, grill the prawns for 4 to 5 minutes, turning halfway through, then drizzle with a little olive oil. Place the grilled prawns on top of the tagine along with a handful of coriander.

Serve the tagine with the couscous, yoghurt and wedges of lemon (use the one you zested) to squeeze over the seafood.

PREPARATION TIME: 10 MINUTES | COOKING TIME: 25-30 MINUTES | SERVES 4

RICHARD HAWARD'S OYSTERS

BY GEMMA TIDMARSH

"The methods we employ in the present day have barely altered in nearly 300 years. The Haward family have been farming oysters for all that time with patience and care at the heart of their business."

Richard Haward's Oysters is based on Mersea Island in Essex and is one of the oldest oyster farming families in the world. The eighth generation, brothers Tom and Bram, are directors of the business with their father, Richard, at the helm. These three are at the core of the business and keep the day to day operations running smoothly.

In 1732, Richard's fourth great grandfather began cultivating oysters from the creeks and marshes of Mersea Island. Since then, the torch has been handed down through the generations and Richard Haward's Oysters now supply oysters to some of the best restaurants in England and export them globally.

As a business, we're extremely passionate about representing the community we're from and showcasing our wonderful products. We produce the rock oyster (Latin name Gigas) and the native oyster. The native oyster has been around for centuries and it is thought that the Romans said they were the only good thing to come out of England! Both types of oysters grow on our fourteen acres of oyster beds which filter water containing the rich nutrients from the surrounding marshland. The oyster industry is governed by the ebb and flow of the tide so we either use our dredging boat, the Jacqueline Anne, to catch our stock or we pick oysters by hand at low tide.

Not only do we grow and supply oysters to various top-end restaurants in the UK, we also have a retail unit at Borough Market, London, which is an internationally renowned foodie hub, where people can buy some of the best fresh produce in the UK including our oysters. Customers are able to get oysters freshly shucked in front of them and slurp a plate of oysters complemented by a glass of fizz.

The methods we employ in the present day have barely altered in nearly 300 years. The Haward family have been farming oysters for all that time with patience and care at the heart of their business. Mersea Island is a beautiful place and our produce is just one example of this fantastic area.

The
COMPANY
SHED

Seafood Platters
Fresh Crab
Mersea Oysters
Our Own Smoked Salmon
Jellied Eels
Fresh King Scallops
Cockles & Prawns
Beetroot Cured Gravadlax
Tiger Prawns
and so much more... COME IN!
thecompanyshed.co

RED SNAPPER OYSTERS WITH PICKLED CELERY

I chose this recipe as it makes the perfect appetiser or canapé for a party. A Red Snapper is like a Bloody Mary but made with gin instead of vodka. We use our own oysters and a gin that's distilled near Mersea Island. — Gemma Tidmarsh

6 celery sticks

125ml cider vinegar

1 tbsp sugar

Large handful of crushed ice

1.25 litres tomato juice

300ml dry gin

3 tbsp lemon juice

2 tbsp Worcestershire sauce

2 tbsp Tabasco

1 tsp horseradish

Ground black pepper

Pinch of Maldon sea salt

8 rock (gigas) oysters

1 lemon, zested

Firstly, you will need to pickle the celery to put on top of the dressed oysters. Finely dice 2 of the 6 celery sticks and place in a bowl. Cover with the cider vinegar and sugar. Stir thoroughly then leave the celery to pickle for 1 hour.

Now you need to make the Red Snappers. This recipe will make 4 drinks and enough left over to dress 8 oysters. Don't make these until the celery has had time to pickle and you're ready to enjoy the oysters. They're the perfect drink to accompany them, especially with a local gin: we use a locally distilled gin called 'The Oysterman'. You will also need a cocktail shaker or a jug.

Put the crushed ice, tomato juice, gin, lemon juice, Worcestershire sauce, Tabasco, horseradish, black pepper and sea salt into the cocktail shaker or jug. Shake to mix everything thoroughly.

Add more crushed ice to 4 glasses then pour the Red Snapper mixture over the top. You will have the equivalent of 1 glass remaining to dress the oysters. Trim the 4 remaining celery sticks and place one in each glass.

Now it is time to shuck your oysters. Once you have shucked them, drizzle them with the remaining Red Snapper mixture and top with the pickled celery, lemon zest and some cracked black pepper. Serve on a bed of seaweed and ice and wash them down with a Red Snapper!

PREPARATION TIME: I HOUR (INCLUDING PICKLING) | SERVES 4 (WE WOULD SUGGEST AT LEAST 2 OYSTERS PER PERSON)

ROB EDLIN

"I enjoy all types of fishing, but always for food rather than sport as I like to catch something that I can eat! It's a hobby that has branched out into lots of other interests, including making my own lobster pots and smoking fish at home."

I enjoy all types of fishing, but always for food rather than sport as I like to catch something that I can eat! It's a hobby that has branched out into lots of other interests, including making my own lobster pots and smoking fish at home, and I have a commercial skipper qualification as well. I usually go out when the weather's good with a few friends who are also skippers, and we know a lot of the commercial fishermen too, so everybody looks out for each other.

My boats are moored on the Helford River and my wife and I live in Lizard, the UK mainland's most southerly village. One of the older fishermen here taught me to make willow lobster pots and I plan to learn how to make hemp rope next, as well as replacing the plastic buoys with locally made blown-glass floats, so the whole thing will be made with natural, biodegradable materials just as it was a hundred years ago. I like keeping these ancient crafts alive, because there's so few people left who know them (and most of them have at least 30 years on me!) but I also use my lobster pots for fishing all year round.

Alongside the lobsters we catch crabs, crawfish, and lots of other shellfish. Most species are very seasonal; between February and April, for example, we go out to wrecks and deeper reefs for pollock, and around November it's mainly squid, mackerel and ling. When I can catch decent-sized herring, they usually get turned into kippers with my other hobby of smoking fish at home. I built a small set up with a shed and cold smoke generator, and we also have an outdoor pizza oven for hot smoking. Any oily fish works well and we make all sorts with them, from pâté to curry.

I want to start offering courses and experiences that show people how to catch and cook fish, and we have recently set up a website that serves as a guide to the South West Coast and our area in general. For me it's about getting out there, experiencing the landscape in the fresh air, and working on the boats - whether we're fishing, repairing or just having a quiet pint afterwards - it's a huge part of life for me.

CRISPY WHITING BURGER WITH CHILLI MAYO

A super easy, fresh and tasty fish burger. It doesn't have to be made with whiting but it's a very sustainable fish that's easy to catch. This is my wife Andrea's recipe as she usually whips up a great dish with whatever I bring home from a day at sea. – Rob Edlin

300g (2-4) fresh skinned whiting fillets (any white fish such as pollock, cod, haddock or hake also works)

For the batter

20g plain flour, plus extra for dusting

55g cornflour

Pinch of salt

Pinch of black pepper

60ml very cold sparkling water

Vegetable oil (enough to cook the fish in a wok or deep pan)

For the chilli mayo

2 tbsp mayonnaise

1 tbsp chilli oil

½ lime, zested and juiced

To serve

2 burger baps

Lettuce leaves

To prepare the fish

If you have fillets with skins on, remove them before cooking. Cut each fillet into evenly-sized pieces so they are just long enough to poke out from the burger bap. Ideally, have two or three of them for each burger.

To make the batter

Mix the flours together with the salt and pepper, then whisk the chilled sparkling water into the seasoned flours to make a smooth batter. The batter should be thick enough to coat the fish: too thick and the batter won't cook enough, too thin and it will slip off the fish when you cook it. Adjust the thickness of the batter with more or less water (start with just a small amount).

For the chilli mayo

Mix the mayonnaise, chilli oil, lime zest and juice together in a small bowl with a fork. Add more lime juice if you prefer a runnier sauce and adjust the amount of chilli oil to your own taste.

To cook the fish

Put the vegetable oil in your pan on the heat. A wok works better because the fish can spread out more. To test whether the oil is hot enough, drop a bit of batter into the hot oil: it should sizzle and rise to the top. The key is to have the oil hot enough to fry the batter and fish quickly, but not too hot to burn them. If you have a thermometer, you can check the temperature which should be around 180 to 190°c.

Coat each fish fillet in the extra plain flour and then dip them in the batter. Carefully place each fillet in the hot oil and cook for 4 to 6 minutes. The batter will be pale with just a tinge of colour. Remove the cooked fish and drain off any oil by placing it on a wire rack or kitchen towel.

Serve the crispy whiting immediately in a burger bap with lettuce, drizzled with the chilli mayo. Add a finely chopped red chilli and a glug of chilli oil for an extra kick if you like.

ROYAL NATIONAL LIFEBOAT INSTITUTION

BY MARK DOWIE

"Our charity has an incredibly strong link with the fishing industry; not only does it go to the aid of fishermen, but they have always formed a large part of our crews. Today our lifeboat stations around the coasts of the UK and Ireland see roughly 10,000 emergency call outs every year."

The RNLI is 197 years old, and for all that time it's been going to the aid of people who work at sea. Our charity has an incredibly strong link with the fishing industry; not only does it go to the aid of fishermen, but they have always formed a large part of our crews. Today, our lifeboat stations around the coasts of the UK and Ireland see roughly 10,000 emergency call outs every year. There are many more incidents in the summer when a lot of people enjoy being at the coast, but a steady flow continues throughout winter and these tend to be commercial in nature because the brave people of the fishing industry go out in all weathers.

My personal association with the sea goes back a long way; I've been a Naval Officer and am a keen sailor as well as Chief Executive of the RNLI. I started as a volunteer at my local lifeboat station in Salcombe; there's very much a sense of community here and if you love the sea, it's an obvious place to be. I also love eating fish and seafood so that's a great part of living by the coast because it's always fresh and seasonal. Salcombe has a crab fishing fleet and the local fishermen are a big part of the town. At the RNLI we work with them, and the lifeboat will typically go out to one or two of the fleet every year.

It's important to remember the RNLI is a charity, funded solely by voluntary donations. That's a very unusual position to be in as an emergency service, but we're proudly independent. The first ever charity street collection took place on behalf of the RNLI in 1891. In more recent times, we have established our annual yellow-themed Mayday fundraiser and our Fish Supper campaign which runs every October, partly to support the fishing industry and remind people ashore how seafood gets onto their plates.

Fishing is one of the most dangerous industries in the UK because the sea is such an unpredictable domain. Throughout the RNLI's history there have been more than 600 crew who have lost their lives in service. Many of these brave crew would have been fishermen, so the RNLI feels it owes a debt to the fishing industry, and the industry relies on the RNLI to continue saving lives at sea.

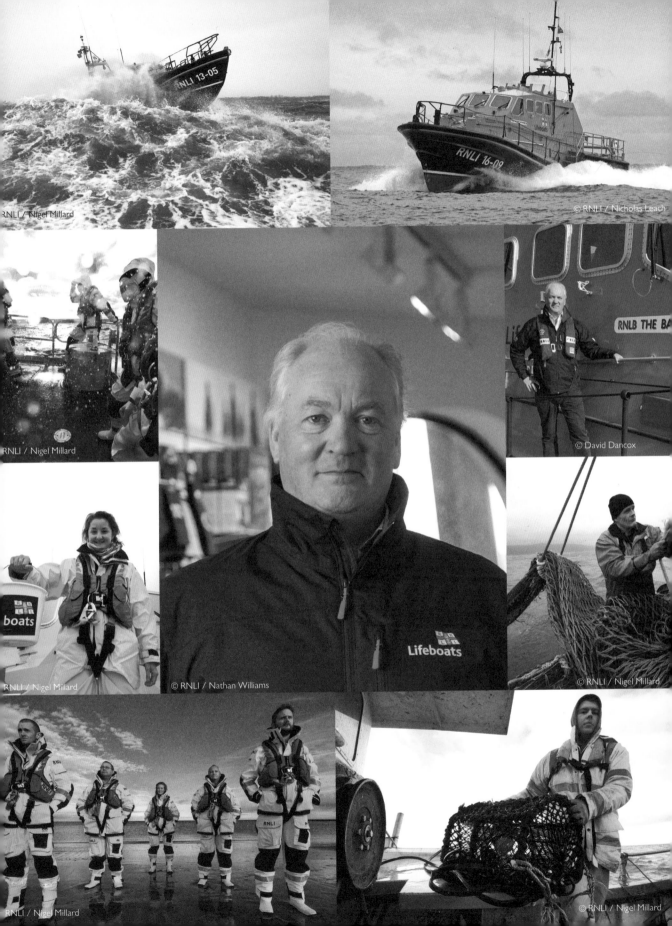

RNLI / Nigel Millard

© RNLI / Nicholas Leach

RNLI / Nigel Millard

© David Dancox

RNLB THE BA

boats

RNLI / Nigel Millard

© RNLI / Nathan Williams

© RNLI / Nigel Millard

RNLI / Nigel Millard

© RNLI / Nigel Millard

BAKED DEVILLED CRAB

· ·

I live near Salcombe, which is famous for its lifeboat, shellfish and gin. This delicious starter can be prepared in advance of any dinner. While you're eating, give a thought to the crab potters who catch shellfish year-round in all weathers, and to the lifeboat crews who keep them safe. — Mark Dowie

450g fresh white and brown crab meat

¼ tsp cayenne pepper

1 tsp Worcestershire sauce

1 tsp lemon juice (freshly squeezed)

1 tsp Dijon mustard

2 tsp anchovy essence

2 tbsp chopped fresh parsley

150ml double cream or crème fraîche

Salt and pepper

1 tsp brandy (optional)

½ tsp horseradish (optional)

2 tbsp grated Parmesan cheese

2 tbsp breadcrumbs (fresh or dried)

You can make this mixture 2 or 3 days ahead, then cover and refrigerate it until needed for an even quicker starter. Otherwise, preheat the oven to 200°c.

Mix the crab meat with the cayenne, Worcestershire sauce, lemon juice, mustard, anchovy essence, parsley and cream or crème fraîche. Add salt and pepper to taste.

Check the seasoning; it should be quite spicy. If you like, add the brandy and horseradish for extra zing!

Divide the crab mixture equally between 6 ramekins. Each one should have about 100ml of mixture, so if the ramekins are small they should be filled to the top. Sprinkle each one with the grated parmesan and breadcrumbs.

Place the ramekins in the preheated oven and bake for 7 to 10 minutes until golden brown. Serve the baked devilled crab with crusty bread on the side.

The original recipe is from The Get-Ahead Cook by Jane Lovett which I've slightly adapted here.

PREPARATION TIME: 10-15 MINUTES | COOKING TIME: 7-10 MINUTES | SERVES 6 AS A STARTER

SALCOMBE ANGLING/ A FISHY BUSINESS

BY CHRIS ROBERTS

"It's important to be able to diversify in this industry, giving yourself as many options as possible to find work in every season. Between April and October, I bring in about 150 lobster pots a day, and we're also very lucky to have a really good scallop fishery right in Salcombe Harbour."

I was born and bred in Salcombe, so I know it like the back of my hand. I've always fished, but decided to make the hobby a profession after working on a boat in Australia. I came back home to pursue the career, got all my qualifications, and now own two boats that go out regularly throughout the year. One is a charter angler for taking people out fishing, which runs mostly during the summer under the name Salcombe Angling. You're pretty much guaranteed to catch your tea around here because the area has great tides and you get into deep water over banks, reefs and wrecks very quickly which is always a bonus, so there's a chance of catching all sorts.

My smaller boat is used for catching bass, mackerel, pollock and other species we can get sustainably using rod and line fishing. It's important to be able to diversify in this industry, giving yourself as many options as possible to find work in every season. Between April and October, I bring in about 150 lobster pots a day, and we're also very lucky to have a really good scallop fishery right in Salcombe Harbour. For the quietest months of the year, December to March, I'm out there Monday to Friday and can earn a fair wage by the end of the week. Everything's done by hand for the scallops; you're not allowed to use haulers because it would damage the seabed so it's heavy work!

All my fish go straight on ice and are gutted straight away if needed, so they're super fresh and well looked after, which fetches a better price and of course makes them all taste so much better. We sell a lot locally in summer months, both directly to restaurants and in the shop run by me and my partner, Sophie Horton. A Fishy Business has tanks to showcase our live crabs and lobsters, which are especially popular with tourists, alongside the fresh fish counters.

For us, it's paramount that everything we sell is as fresh as possible. The taste of a mackerel or bass caught that day by rod and line is totally different to a supermarket fish. Seafood has to be looked after: the more care you take, the better the end result for the customers, the fishermen and the environments we rely on.

BARBECUED LING OR POLLOCK

·····································

Ling is a really underrated fish. It tastes great and we catch a lot, but it's not widely available. The market price is really low so it's good value if you can find it. A good fishmonger might be able to get it, but pollock is a nice alternative if not. — Chris Roberts

5-6 spring onions, chopped

2 fillets of ling or pollock

Knob of butter

Salt and pepper, to taste

Sprinkle the chopped spring onions over the fillets of fish, then wrap them in tin foil with a knob of butter. Place the parcel on the barbecue to cook the fish in the butter and its own juices. Ling is a juicy, thick fish, so it doesn't want to be done in a flash but needs to be cooking for 20 minutes or perhaps a bit more. If you're using pollock, it doesn't take quite as long but should also be cooked slowly at medium heat.

Alternatively, the wrapped fillets can be cooked in the oven at a moderate heat or even, if the fillets aren't too thick, just in a hot frying pan with a little oil until opaque and flaky but still juicy.

Personally, we never like to over complicate our fish. We feel as though sauces often take away the whole idea of what the fish is, and we want to taste the fish, not the sauce.

If this recipe is being made in the summer, we suggest serving it with a nice chopped salad and a little homemade dressing, to enhance the freshness of the fish. In autumn, new potatoes (we like Jersey Royals) are a great addition to the plate along with some peas and fresh mint.

Occasionally, Sophie makes chips which also go well with the ling or pollock but as a general rule we don't deep fry, and certainly never chuck any of our fish (except perhaps squid) in batter!

PREPARATION TIME: 5 MINUTES | COOKING TIME: 20-30 MINUTES | SERVES 2

THE SCOTTISH ASSOCIATION FOR MARINE SCIENCE

BY DR ADAM HUGHES

"Here on the west coast of Scotland we have a vibrant aquaculture industry, and as a researcher it is a privilege to collaborate with an industry so committed to producing high quality products. I am always astounded by the care, attention and dedication that goes into producing our seafood."

I've lived by the sea ever since we moved from Scotland down to the south coast of England when I was young. As children, we would always be at the beach. I remember being woken up early on school mornings throughout the year to walk the dogs and go for a swim before school, if the weather was good.

I wasn't particularly academic at school and chose to do a lot of vocational courses, including cooking, so I guess I'm really lucky that my current job combines both my love for the ocean and my deep interest and appreciation of food. When we were growing up, we never ate fish; neither of my parents knew how to cook it. It wasn't until I left home and started travelling as an itinerant marine biologist that I got to experience great seafood. I've been privileged to live and work with coastal communities in Tanzania, Mozambique, Fiji and the Bahamas, where seafood is a staple, freshly caught and served simply.

After I stopped travelling and came to Scotland to do my PhD, moving into a career that allowed me to work both in the world of food and marine science was a natural step, and so I evolved into a researcher and lecturer in sustainable aquaculture at SAMS. Aquaculture can be a contentious issue, but as we face the challenges of feeding upwards of nine billion people in the future, we have to recognise that farming the seas and oceans needs to play an important part in providing food, both globally and locally.

Here on the west coast of Scotland we have a vibrant aquaculture industry, and as a researcher it is a privilege to collaborate with an industry so committed to producing high quality products. I am always astounded by the care, attention and dedication that goes into producing our seafood. All food production has an environmental impact when done at scale, and much of my work is based on reducing that impact, while maintaining the social and economic sustainability of the industry.

The Scottish Association for Marine Science (SAMS) is Scotland's largest and oldest independent marine science organisation, delivering marine science for a productive and sustainably managed marine environment through innovative research, education and engagement with society.

MUSSELS WITH SEAWEED

· ·

I chose this recipe because the two main ingredients are sustainably farmed, and perfect for the waters off Scotland where I live and work. The combination of mussels and seaweed is also absolutely delicious, with real depth of flavour, delivering a delicious and nutritious twist on the classic moules marinière. — Dr Adam Hughes

5-10g dried dulse seaweed

600-700g Scottish rope-grown mussels

2 tbsp olive oil

1 small onion or shallot

Freshly ground black pepper

100ml dry cider

40g unsalted butter, cubed

Place the dried seaweed in a bowl with fresh water to allow it to rehydrate. For this version I used the red seaweed, dulse, which can be purchased from whole food shops in the dried form. Because it has a robust flavour I add some during the cooking, but if you are using more delicately flavoured seaweeds it could perhaps be added later as a garnish.

Just before cooking, clean the mussels by placing them in a bowl with fresh water, scraping the shells to remove any barnacles, and removing any beards. Discard any shells that are open. Drain and rinse the mussels once cleaned.

Heat the olive oil in a decent size pan with a good lid. Peel and finely dice the onion or shallot, then add it to the oil and cook on a medium heat until just beginning to turn golden.

While the onion is cooking, remove the seaweed from the water and squeeze dry. Slice it into fine ribbons with a sharp knife. When the onion is ready, add half of the seaweed and a good amount of black pepper to taste, then continue frying for another couple of minutes.

Turn up the heat, add the mussels to the pan and stir well to mix everything together. Add the cider, cover with the lid and leave to steam for 4 to 5 minutes until all the shells have opened. Give the pan a shake or a good stir a couple of times during cooking.

Place a colander or sieve in a bowl and tip the contents of the pan into the colander, collecting the juices in the bowl. Set the mussels aside briefly and return the juices to the original pan. Heat until simmering, then add the butter and whisk until it melts into the sauce. At this point, keeping the pan on the heat, add the mussels, the rest of the seaweed and more black pepper. Replace the lid and cook for 30 seconds to 1 minute, until the sauce is simmering again, while stirring well. Serve from the pan, ladling the mussels and sauce into bowls, accompanied by freshly baked bread.

SCOTTISH SHELLFISH

· ·

BY STEPHEN CAMERON

"As a co-op, Scottish Shellfish works with shared goals and a common interest. We invest as much as we can back into the farmers, providing equipment to help them do their jobs while letting their expertise show us the way forward."

Scottish Shellfish is a co-op that began as individual mussel and oyster farmers who came together to get everyone's produce into restaurants. It's led by myself and Rob Mitchell, our commercial director, alongside the board of shellfish farmers. Our purpose-built factory near Glasgow allows us to efficiently process and supply their products to consumers across the nation, and our farms now stretch the length of mainland Scotland and the Shetland Isles.

Our mussels are carefully cultivated in the pristine seas off the Scottish west coast and Shetland. Michael Tait, chairman of the Scottish Shellfish Board, is also one of the farmers:

"Shetland Mussels was established in 1997 by my father, my brother and I. Selling wholesale in small volumes was time consuming, so we joined Scottish Shellfish in 2009. We now produce over 2000 tonnes per year, have taken on more sites and employed more people, so the co-op gave us that potential for growth too. For me, the really positive thing about mussel farming is that it's an environmentally friendly form of aquaculture; we hope to have a low carbon footprint in the future. It can also generate a good income in rural areas of Scotland. The work is challenging, no doubt about it, but the quality of the end product definitely makes it worthwhile."

Gordon Turnbull, from Isle of Mull Oysters, explains how his sector of aquaculture works:

"We buy the Pacific oysters from seed and spend the next three to four years growing them above the seabed on the foreshore. As it's an underwater farm, we can only access the oysters for two or three hours a day every second week, so the work is very intense. Not many people do it, but you get out what you put in and I enjoy it. What the co-operative does is really allow us to concentrate on running the farm. Everybody on the board has a rural, coastal farm so there's a lot in common and they understand where you're coming from. There's a strong feeling that we're all pushing together rather than working competitively, especially in difficult times."

As a co-op, Scottish Shellfish works with shared goals and a common interest. We invest as much as we can back into the farmers, providing equipment to help them do their jobs while letting their expertise show us the way forward.

GRILLED OYSTERS WITH GARLIC BUTTER

Our locally grown oysters are delicious cooked with garlic, velvety butter and fresh cracked black pepper, paired with zingy lemon. The perfect weekend starter treat.
– Stephen Cameron

3 tbsp unsalted butter, softened

2 tbsp olive oil

2 cloves of garlic, grated

1 tbsp very finely chopped fresh parsley

Squeeze of lemon juice

Dash of Tabasco

Cracked black pepper

8 whole live oysters

In a bowl, mix the butter with the oil, garlic, parsley, lemon juice, Tabasco and some black pepper to taste. Place the closed oysters on a baking tray with the flat side of the shell facing upwards. Place under a preheated grill for 1 minute. When you start to see the shells opening, remove them from the grill.

Using an oven mitt to protect your hands from the heat, slide a shucking knife or a sturdy round-bladed knife into the gap between the top and bottom of the shell. Twist the knife to lever the shell open. Remove the top of the shell and place the oyster in the bottom half of the shell back on the tray.

Repeat this with all the oysters, then divide the sauce between the shells and grill for another 2 to 3 minutes. Remove the oysters from the grill, place them onto a large plate and serve with a crisp salad and lemon wedges.

THE SEAFOOD SHACK

BY FENELLA RENWICK

"We get to cook all summer long, looking over towards the mountains on the other side of the loch, we can interact with our amazing customers each day, and most importantly we don't have the pressures of a huge business, so we can still have fun!"

Originally from Achmore, I have worked in catering and seafood for a number of years and my family have businesses in the fishing industry and seafood. I believe that the seafood here in Ullapool is some of the best in the world and I love being able to share it with others. My business partner, Kirsty Scobie, was born and raised in Ullapool and has worked in catering and seafood for a number of years. Her family still live in and around Ullapool and her partner owns one of the local boats and lands much of what is served here at The Seafood Shack.

We opened The Seafood Shack in May 2016 and have been thriving ever since. It's a catering trailer providing simple, quick and delicious seafood cooked to order. We source all our produce locally which helps our local businesses and community, and also ensures that everything we serve is fresh. We decided that both being in our mid-twenties, a restaurant was a bit of a daunting task and, truthfully, didn't appeal. We thought that a seafood catering trailer would be perfect and it really is. We get to cook all summer long, looking over towards the mountains on the other side of the loch, we can interact with our amazing customers each day, and most importantly we don't have the pressures of a huge business, so we can still have fun!

Ullapool was an ideal location to set up our business. It has some of the best seafood in Scotland, from live lobsters to fresh haddock. The town also has many inshore fishing boats that come in to land throughout the year. The produce from these boats wasn't getting used to its full potential, and a high percentage was leaving Ullapool, so for us this was a huge gap in the market. Each morning the fishermen drop off their catch of the day and we create a daily menu depending on what we have in. This keeps us and our customers on their toes!

Since opening in 2016 we have had great opportunities and won multiple awards for our service. Some of these include being featured in the great Mary Berry's Everyday Life series in 2017, being named Best Eating Experience 2018 in the Highlands and Islands Tourism Awards, and winning the Jane Grigson Trust Award for new food writers in 2020.

THE
SEAFOOD
SHACK

THE
SEAFOOD
SHACK

Photos and recipe from The Seafood Shack – Food and Tales From Ullapool
by Kirsty Scobie and Fenella Renwick, published by Kitchen Press.

MOROCCAN LANGOUSTINE RICE

This is a great dish for a dinner party; it's not too difficult to make and is almost a one-pot wonder. If you feel like you want something on the side, serve it with a big fresh salad. — Fenella Renwick

24 cooked langoustines

1 bay leaf

½ lemon, juiced

Salt and pepper

50g butter

Glug of vegetable or rapeseed oil

1 white onion, finely chopped

2 cloves of garlic, finely chopped

½ red chilli, thinly sliced

1cm fresh ginger, peeled and grated

3 spring onions, trimmed and chopped

1 x 400g tin of chickpeas, drained and rinsed

Handful of green beans, ends trimmed

2 tsp paprika

1 tsp ground cumin

1 tsp ground coriander

1 tsp ground turmeric

200g basmati rice

4 tbsp crème fraîche

Peel the cooked langoustines, then pop the shells in a large saucepan and the meat in the fridge for later. Cover the shells with at least twice as much water and add the bay leaf, lemon juice and a good grind of black pepper. Bring to the boil, turn the heat down and simmer with a lid on for at least 30 minutes to make a stock for your rice to cook in later. If you don't have time to make langoustine stock for your rice, don't worry. Just cook the rice as instructed on the packet and save your shells for another day.

Place a frying pan on a high heat and add the butter and oil. Once it's melted, turn the heat down to medium and add the onion, garlic, chilli, ginger and half of the spring onions. Sweat them for about 10 minutes on a low heat, making sure nothing burns. Stir in your chickpeas, green beans, paprika, cumin, coriander and turmeric. Cook for another 5 minutes, then remove from the heat.

Rinse the basmati rice in cold water until the water runs clear. Drain your langoustine stock through a fine sieve into a big bowl and pour about a litre of the stock into a saucepan. Pop it back on the heat and bring to the boil, then add the rice and simmer for 8 minutes so the rice still has a bite to it. Drain the rice in a sieve when done.

Place your chickpea mixture back on the heat, then stir in the reserved langoustine meat and the drained rice. Cook, stirring gently, until everything is piping hot. If it looks too dry, add a splash of stock to loosen the sauce until it has a good consistency.

Season the Moroccan langoustine rice with salt and pepper to taste, sprinkle it with the remaining spring onions, then serve with a dollop of crème fraîche for each person.

SOLE BAY FISH COMPANY

BY DARREN MARRIOTT

"In 2013, Mother Nature changed the way we were to operate. A phenomenal flood caused by a tidal surge led me to redevelop the business, creating what is here today. In the serene surroundings of the new restaurant, visitors can choose from a plethora of locally sourced, fresh, well-cooked fish and shellfish."

Sole Bay Fish Company was created in 1999 by myself, a born fisherman from Mersea Island in Colchester. It all began with a single shed on Southwold Harbour to sell the fresh fish caught daily from my own boat, Our Carol II. Over time, the shed has developed into the beautiful fishmongers you see today which continues to sell an abundance of fresh fish, ready to eat shellfish and smoked products.

In 2006 I started serving chilled seafood platters in a small seating area by the fishmongers. Popularity grew over a 'Bring Your Own' liquid refreshment and bread theme while enjoying the shellfish platters made to order. In 2013, Mother Nature changed the way we were to operate. A phenomenal flood caused by a tidal surge led me to redevelop the business, creating what is here today. In the serene surroundings of the new restaurant, visitors can choose from a plethora of locally sourced, fresh, well-cooked fish and shellfish.

In 2015 Sole Bay was expanded to include the Little Fish & Chip Shop takeaway service in Southwold High Street. Fresh fish is cooked to order in traditional beef dripping and served with twice cooked chips, giving them a crisp texture.

Sole Bay's newest venture is an oyster farm on the River Blyth, growing rock oysters to sell on the wet fish counter and serve in my restaurant. Another recent addition to Sole Bay is the Suzie P, a fishing boat captained by my son. Alongside Our Carol II, it lands rock, rays, soles and bass to serve in my restaurant.

The Sole Bay Fish Company family welcomes everyone, and we are very proud of the dine-in options at our comfortable restaurant, the abundant choice from the fishmongers, and the convenient takeaway service from the traditional Little Fish & Chip Shop here in Southwold.

LUXURY BREADED SOLE BAY FISHCAKE

Our homemade fishcake is unique and was invented to avoid wastage from the fishmonger counter. The recipe has evolved over a number of years and the version below is considered to be the best! – Darren Marriot

1kg desiree potatoes (peeled and cooked weight 800g)

Sea salt

Ground white pepper

200g cod fillet, skinless and boneless

100g smoked undyed haddock fillet, skinned and boneless

100g Greenland peeled prawns, defrosted

1 litre ice-cold water

Self-raising flour

300g panko breadcrumbs

Wash, peel and re-wash the potatoes and then cut into large chunks. Cover the potatoes with cold water in a suitable pan and add a good pinch of salt. Gently bring to the boil and simmer for 18 minutes. Drain the potatoes thoroughly. If they still have a lot of excess moisture, place the potatoes in a shallow tray and bake in the oven for approximately 15 to 20 minutes on a low heat to dry them out. Mash the potatoes while hot and add a pinch of ground white pepper.

While the potatoes are cooking, cut the fish fillets into evenly-sized pieces and place in a shallow tray with a splash of water in the bottom to prevent the fish from sticking. Cover with tin foil and bake in the oven for 15 minutes at 160°c or 140°c fan. When the fish is cooked, drain off any excess liquid.

Combine the mashed potato, cooked fish and peeled prawns gently, so that you can see flakes of fish throughout the mixture. Divide the mixture into 150g portions and mould using a burger press into approximately 8 fishcakes. Tip: Cover the base of the burger press in cling film to prevent the fishcake mix from sticking. Place the fishcakes in the fridge to set while you prepare the batter and breadcrumbs.

Put the ice-cold water in a large bowl and whisk in enough self-raising flour to produce a batter the consistency of double cream. Place the panko breadcrumbs in a separate bowl ready to coat your fishcakes. Dip each fishcake into the batter first, allowing any excess to drain off, then lay it in the breadcrumbs. Lightly pat the fishcake before turning over and repeating the process on the other side. Gently roll the edges of the fishcake in the breadcrumbs before placing it on a tray lined with greaseproof paper. Repeat with all the fishcakes, then place the tray in the fridge until required or cover with cling film and freeze for a later date.

To cook, place the fishcakes on an oiled baking tray and drizzle over a little sunflower oil. Place them in a preheated oven at 180°c or 160°c fan for 20 minutes, turning halfway through. If cooking the fishcakes from frozen, increase the cooking time to 40 minutes.

Ensure the fishcakes are piping hot throughout, and serve with chips or a side salad, tartare sauce and a wedge of lemon.

STAR CASTLE HOTEL

· ·

BY ROBERT FRANCIS

"In the early mornings, weather permitting, I take my boat out to sea to haul, check and re-bait my lobster pots and crawfish nets, that – if my luck is in – will contain a good mix of lobsters, crabs and crawfish."

Living and working on the Isles of Scilly, life is all about the sea. This is just as it has been for most of my life, as a born and bred Cornishman, and now an Islander. Here on Scilly, I am blessed to be able to channel my love of fishing directly into the running of our historic hotel, the sixteenth century Star Castle, which stands on the garrison of St Mary's, the largest island in this glorious archipelago off the coast of Cornwall.

In the early mornings, weather permitting, I take my boat out to sea to haul, check and re-bait my lobster pots and crawfish nets, that – if my luck is in – will contain a good mix of lobsters, crabs and crawfish. Guests at the hotel have first dibs on the catch, with opportunities to enjoy a fresh lobster thermidor for dinner or a beautifully prepared savoury tart, like the crawfish one featured over the page. If we've had a good harvest, they might wash it down with a glass or two of chilled chardonnay, produced at our own HolyVale Vineyard just a stone's throw from the Castle.

At the Castle and the vineyard, we serve a 'one mile lobster lunch' during the summer months, which combines freshly caught lobster, potatoes and salad from our kitchen garden and wine from our own grapes, all grown no more than a mile away from each other. Diners at the Castle can choose between our two restaurants, with seafood dominating the Conservatory menu and meat – sourced almost exclusively from Cornwall – served in the Castle. There's always a couple of delicious vegetarian options on each menu, too, making good use of the produce grown in the very temperate climate that we enjoy year-round across the islands.

My son, James, is responsible for the smooth running of both restaurants and the hotel, leaving me to indulge my follies of fishing and wine. Head chef Billy Littlejohn works tirelessly with sous chef Richard Matthews, Simon Shaw and the rest of the kitchen team to produce daily changing menus for each restaurant, with a focus on freshly made, locally sourced, beautifully nuanced menus that reflect the seasons, both on the land and in the sea that surrounds this wonderful place we call home.

Photos © Chris Hall Photography

CARAMELISED ONION TART WITH SCILLONIAN CRAWFISH, ROCK SAMPHIRE AND CHIVE HOLLANDAISE

A very simple but fresh and tasty dish showcasing the Scillonian crawfish that is caught by myself, the hotel owner. The crawfish is delivered within 5 minutes from the holding pot to ensure absolute freshness. — Robert Francis

For the caramelised onion tart

8 large onions

75g unsalted butter

Salt and pepper

1 tsp thyme leaves

300g puff pastry

For the crawfish and samphire

500g fresh crawfish

2.5 litres water

1 cup of salt

20g rock samphire

10g butter

For the chive hollandaise

1 tbsp white wine vinegar

50ml cold water

½ tbsp white peppercorns, crushed

4 egg yolks

200g clarified butter

½ lemon, juiced

Pinch of salt

Handful of chives, chopped

For the caramelised onion tart

Halve the onions and cut each half into thin slices. Melt the butter in a frying pan over a high heat. Add the onions to the pan, cover with a lid and leave them to cook for 5 minutes until softened. Stir the onions and season with salt and pepper. Turn the heat down low and add the thyme leaves. Continue to sweat the onions until they are pale golden and sweet.

Preheat the oven to 200°c. Roll out the puff pastry, cut into 3 by 12cm rectangles and prick each with a fork several times. Place the rectangles on baking trays, leaving enough room between each to allow for expanding. Spread the caramelised onions evenly on the pastry rectangles, leaving a 0.5cm gap on the long side. Bake the tarts in the preheated oven for 20 minutes.

When baked, remove them from the oven and place each tart on the cooling rack, leaving them to rest for 5 minutes.

For the crawfish and samphire

First, humanely dispatch the crawfish. Bring the water to the boil in a large saucepan, add the salt and the crawfish and simmer for 10 to 12 minutes. When cooked, plunge the crawfish into iced water. Once cooled, remove the tail meat ready to serve. Wash the samphire then cook it in the butter in a hot frying pan for 1 minute.

For the chive hollandaise

Combine the white wine vinegar, water and crushed pepper in a small pan over a medium heat. Reduce by a third and then leave to cool off the heat. Once cooled, add the egg yolks and place the pan back on a gentle heat, whisking continuously. Slowly increase the heat until the mixture becomes smooth and creamy; this usually takes 8 to 10 minutes. Remove from the heat, still whisking, and add the cold clarified butter. Pass the sauce through a fine sieve and add the lemon juice, salt and chives to taste. Serve as soon as possible.

To serve

Gently warm the onion tarts under the grill. Heat the crawfish and samphire in a pan with a knob of butter and season to taste. Place the tart in the middle of a plate, top with the crawfish and spoon over the hollandaise. Add the samphire to the plate and serve.

STEPHEN AND SHEILA TAYLOR

....

"We would catch a certain tide, going out Monday to Friday at all times of the day and through the night in the summer which was absolutely beautiful...The air was always so lovely and fresh, although we went in all weathers and you never knew what you were going to catch."

Salmon netting is all gone now, but that's what we did on the River Taw here in North Devon for many years. I'll be 84 soon, and Stephen's 90: it's kept us fit and healthy for a long time! We would catch a certain tide, going out Monday to Friday at all times of the day and through the night in the summer which was absolutely beautiful. Once we saw two otters, the first I'd ever seen, and watched them playing in the river on our way to fish. The air was always so lovely and fresh, although we went in all weathers and you never knew what you were going to catch; sometimes we came back with nothing.

When there was plenty, we'd sell some of our catch to different people - Lady Arran from Castle Hill was a regular - and had a fish shop at Butcher's Row in Barnstaple. Stephen was a salmon fisherman for over 60 years; it was part of his living even when the licences became very difficult to get and expensive too. He first learned to read the moods of the tides and currents out fishing with his uncles in the days when the salmon boats were larger, the nets were heavier and each boat had three crew plus the skipper.

Once upon a time almost everyone living by the Taw or Torridge in North Devon had a boat and tried to catch salmon. Licenses were restricted in the 1800s but the numbers kept falling, for lots of different reasons. In 2002 the riparian owners (the rods men) offered to buy out the remaining nets men on the estuary for £10,000 each. Only three boats refused the money and continued to fish, and one of them was me and Stephen.

I started salmon netting when I met Stephen, and it was very, very enjoyable. We always fished together, pulling the nets in and helping each other get our waterproof trousers on! There's still a lot of salmon in the River Taw but the traditional methods of fishing will die out and the skills will be lost because no one's allowed to have a license any more. It's so sad for me and Stephen because that was a huge part of our life, but that's the way it goes.

SIMPLE SALMON FILLETS

· ·

It's so easy to do a lovely bit of salmon for dinner. Like all fresh fish, it hardly needs any cooking. We live off fish; I go down to Cornwall with my daughter quite often to find the best varieties. It tastes best when you get it yourself! – Sheila Taylor

1 side of salmon (about 100-150g per person)

30g butter

Salt and pepper

1 lemon, halved

Slice the fish into portions of the size you want. Warm up a grill pan with the butter in, then put the salmon fillets into the pan. It should be cooked perfectly after about 5 minutes. Sprinkle some salt and pepper over the fish, then squeeze on some lemon juice to your taste.

You can have whatever you want with this salmon because the flavours are so simple. I like corn on the cob or peas, and you can have any greens on the side. Any kind of potatoes you've got will do; I can't stand mashed potato but a lot of people like that with it!

PREPARATION TIME: 5 MINUTES | COOKING TIME: 5 MINUTES | SERVES 4 OR MORE

THE URBAN FISHWIFE

BY CAROLINE RYE

"We have such a rich fishing heritage; we're an island nation! Yet there are still many barriers when it comes to getting more people enjoying seafood. My aim is to demonstrate how easy and versatile seafood can be."

Some years ago I had the chance to take a sabbatical from my office job and retrain at the world renowned Ballymaloe Cookery School in Ireland, a lifelong dream. There I learnt from amazing teachers and cooked with the finest produce Ireland had to offer. The fish was sustainably caught from local boats and I handled incredible shellfish from tiny periwinkles to prize lobsters.

After Ballymaloe I didn't head straight to the kitchen but worked in the seafood industry for Seafish. As I found out about the challenges of getting people to eat more seafood, the more I thought there was an opportunity to develop a blog specialising in seafood recipes. From there The Urban Fishwife was born. The name was inspired by the famous fishwives of Newhaven, who sold fish from the baskets on their backs door to door.

Since then I've written recipes for the Marine Stewardship Council, the Marine Conservation Society and consumer brand Fish is the Dish. I've also created recipes for the new UK Love Seafood campaign. I provide consultancy too, working on several studies exploring consumer attitudes to seafood, and how to increase seafood consumption. One of my most recent projects has been bringing the Sustainable Fish Cities campaign to Edinburgh, connecting producers with local customers who want to buy sustainable seafood.

I'm a big believer in eating beyond the 'big five' species: salmon, cod, haddock, prawns and tuna. These make up the majority of the seafood we eat in the UK but the waters around us contain many more. One of the ways we can make sustainable choices is by reducing pressure on popular fish stocks and enjoying others instead. I run a regular feature on Instagram called #neptunesbounty, where I cook with different types of seafood to help inspire others to cook with them too.

We have such a rich fishing heritage; we're an island nation! Yet there are still many barriers when it comes to getting more people enjoying seafood. My aim is to demonstrate how easy and versatile seafood can be.

EGGS ÉCOSSE

· ·

This is my take on Eggs Royale, a brunch dish that replaces the usual smoked salmon with smoked whiting. Whiting is a much underused fish but smoking brings out its terrific flavour. Good quality ready-made hollandaise sauce is really handy but feel free to make your own! – Caroline Rye

2 fillets undyed smoked whiting (about 180g each)

20g unsalted butter, plus extra for the toast

2 leeks

2 handfuls of kale, sprout tops or other greens

1 tsp olive oil

4 slices of sourdough bread

1 packet of good quality ready-made hollandaise sauce

2 large organic eggs

Black pepper

2 lemon wedges, to serve

Preheat the oven to 180°c. Wrap the whiting in foil with the unsalted butter, place on a baking tray and bake in the oven for 15 minutes.

Trim and clean the leeks, then thinly slice. Destalk and roughly chop the kale or other greens. Heat the olive oil in a frying pan and fry the vegetables for a few minutes until they start to soften but still have some bite. Set aside.

Boil a pan of water for cooking the eggs. Toast the sourdough bread. Heat the hollandaise sauce gently in a small pan.

Poach the eggs in simmering water for 3 to 4 minutes, then drain them on a clean tea towel. Butter the toast. Remove the whiting from the oven and carefully unwrap the foil.

To serve

Top the toast with the greens, fish, poached eggs and then pour over the sauce. Finish with some black pepper and a squeeze of lemon juice.

PREPARATION TIME: 15 MINUTES | COOKING TIME: 15 MINUTES | SERVES 2

VIN SULLIVAN FOODS

BY CHRIS PARKER

"We promote Welsh seafood where possible, including Pembrokeshire crab and lobsters, laverbread and cockles from Penclawdd, and even wild sea bass from the Gower when it's in season."

Vin Sullivan Foods started as a fishmonger in 1960, and was one of the first to expand in order to supply the whole of the UK with fresh fish and seafood. The original owner has now retired, and the company has been owned by Paul Male since 2018, who also owns Snowden & Co. in Cardiff, Wales' largest fish wholesaler. We're now based in both Blaenavon and Cardiff and our team has over 100 years of experience between us!

I'm the first and currently the only Master Fishmonger in Wales, one of my colleagues has been working here on and off since the age of 14 - he has also won the British Fish Craft Championships twice in that time - and over the years we have produced many other award-winning fishmongers. We train fish counter staff for one of the major retailers, and are heavily involved with the National Federation of Fishmongers, along with other trade groups.

Vin Sullivan has always stocked a wide range of fish and seafood products - along with meat, cheese, game, and a variety of ingredients from our delicatessen - and today you can find pretty much anything in our shop and on the website. We promote Welsh seafood where possible, including Pembrokeshire crab and lobsters, laverbread and cockles from Penclawdd, and even wild sea bass from the Gower when it's in season. We also source fish from all the major UK ports: Shetland mussels; Scottish hake; a variety of species such as lemon sole, red mullet, turbot, gurnard and squid from Cornwall; and cod and haddock from Grimsby.

We've noticed that in recent years, exotic imports have become less popular, and customers across the board, wholesale and public, prefer to buy fish and seafood closer to home. Vin Sullivan supplies hotels, restaurants and caterers across the UK, and we prepare everything to order as required. We also sell online through The Fish Shack, our newest branch of the business which is dedicated to selling fresh fish and seafood direct to the customer.

Our mobile fishmonger goes to markets in Abergavenny and Pontypridd, where people especially love hake and cockles, and stocking homegrown shellfish for those customers is a must. We can also ensure that our standards are met this way, as all the produce they sell comes straight from Vin Sullivan Foods each day. The level of quality and service we offer is the driving force behind the whole business; it's what we were built on and how we'll continue.

FISH SHACK
VIN SULLIVAN

National Federation of Fish Mongers

of Fish Mongers

Welsh Seafood & More to your Door

VIN SULL
Suppliers of fir

VS
ESTD

vin-sullivan.co.uk
01495 792 792

James Davies

LAVERBREAD AND COCKLE FRITTERS

I'm a longstanding friend of Vin Sullivan so was happy to share this easy yet unusual recipe for them; it was always a favourite in their cookery school. Laverbread is a traditional Welsh product made from edible seaweed, and it pairs very well with the delicious savoury flavours of cockles and parmesan. — Chef Franco Taruschio

140g self-raising flour

1 egg

Salt and pepper

30g parmesan, grated

100g laverbread (tinned or fresh)

110-140g shelled cooked cockles

1 litre sunflower or grapeseed oil

Put the flour into a bowl, make a well in the centre and crack in the egg. Add a little water, then whisk the dry ingredients into the liquids until you have a smooth batter. Season with salt and pepper, but don't use a lot because the main ingredients are salty already.

Stir the grated parmesan into your batter, then fold through the laverbread and cockles. Make sure everything is well mixed and there are no lumps of flour left.

Heat the sunflower or grapeseed oil in a large sturdy pan with deep sides. Drop a small piece of batter into the oil to check whether it's at the right temperature to fry without browning too quickly.

Carefully place dessertspoonfuls of the mixture into the hot oil in small batches, turning as needed and removing the fritters when they have a good colour all over. It should take about 6 minutes for them to turn golden. Place them on kitchen paper to absorb the excess oil before serving at once, while the fritters are still hot.

PREPARATION TIME: 10 MINUTES | COOKING TIME: 5-10 MINUTES | SERVES 4

WESTER ROSS FISHERIES

BY BARBORA GABOROVA

"What makes our salmon unique is our ethical and sustainable approach to salmon farming alongside the all-natural health control: priceless cleaner fish, wrasse. We are the guardians of our environment, preserving not only the beautiful craft of salmon rearing, but also the stunning nature around us, for generations to come."

Wester Ross Fisheries is the oldest and only independent salmon farmer in the UK. Our story started back in 1977, when Dr Robin Bradley founded the very first Wester Ross farm by the shores of Ullapool on the west coast of the Scottish Highlands. It is his son, Gilpin Bradley, who now runs the farm with another director, David Robinson. They have both been working on the farms since the 1980s, and in fact, most of our farmers are the second or even third generation. We practice a rare, traditional labour-intensive way of farming the salmon, very much in sync with the natural cycle of wild salmon.

Here at Wester Ross, we grow our salmon slowly to taste delicious. Raised on an organic diet, the salmon are ready to be harvested after two and a half years on the farm. There are no antibiotics, no growth promoters and no GMOs involved at any stage of their life as they are raised in the protected wild environment of the farms. Hand-rearing them takes longer and requires more people, effort and passion, but the outcome is an incredibly flavourful fish full of Omega-3 and good fats that is hard to forget!

We want people to discover the complex flavours of sustainably raised fish and to support their own local sustainable farms and businesses. We love teaching people how to trace their salmon to the point of origin as well as how to cook and treat it right to achieve the best taste and vitamin and protein intake possible. This is an important part of the process, as education creates awareness of the products we consume and appreciation of the work behind each one of them.

Wester Ross Salmon represents the best umami flavours of the Scottish Highlands, preserved in a beautiful light-pink flesh. What makes our salmon unique is our ethical and sustainable approach, alongside the all-natural health control of priceless cleaner fish, wrasse. We are the guardians of our environment, preserving not only the beautiful craft of salmon rearing, but also the stunning nature around us, for generations to come. Our roots are deeply embedded in the Highlands; they are our home. Here at Wester Ross Fisheries, we not only strive to preserve the tradition of salmon farming but also the life of small rural communities so essential for safeguarding one of the biggest treasures of our country, Scottish Atlantic salmon.

SLOW-ROAST CITRUS WESTER ROSS SALMON

This versatile dish is easy enough for midweek meals, but also makes a beautiful centerpiece at the dinner party table. Try adding different herbs and spices to upscale the flavours and make it your own. Leftovers store well and make delicious sandwiches, wraps, pasta dishes and more. — Simon Rodgers

1 tangerine

1 blood orange

1 navel orange, or equivalent

2 lemons

½ fillet of Wester Ross Salmon, skin on or off

Sea salt flakes

Black pepper

6 sprigs of fresh thyme

250ml sustainable cold-pressed rapeseed oil, or pomace olive oil

Handful of fresh parsley

Fennel fronds

Start by preheating the oven to 150°c. Taking care, cut all of the fruit into thin slices, making sure to leave the skins on. Next, season both sides of the salmon generously with the sea salt flakes and black pepper. Sea salt flakes are much more gentle in flavour than sand-like table or cooking salt, so don't be afraid to be generous with it.

Lay out a bed of citrus slices using half of them, making sure there is a variety of all 4 fruits, in the base of a deep ceramic dish along with 3 of the sprigs of thyme. Place the seasoned salmon into the dish and cover with the remaining citrus slices and thyme sprigs.

Generously drizzle the oil over the fruit covering the salmon, then place the dish in the oven for 25 to 35 minutes, until the fish is just cooked. We recommend treating it like a good piece of steak, so the flesh should be slightly pink in the middle. Salmon is best served after resting for 5 minutes. Once rested, garnish the dish with the parsley and fennel fronds.

To serve

This light dish pairs well with a mixed leaf salad, fresh crusty bread for the oils and a glass of local, perfectly chilled white wine in the warmer weather. Try an easy IPA alongside roasted vegetables in the colder months when hearty comfort food is called for. Enjoy!

PREPARATION TIME: 20 MINUTES | COOKING TIME: 25-35 MINUTES | SERVES 4

W. STEVENSON

BY VICTORIA TOWNSEND

"In the UK we have such a wealth of high quality British fish; we should all embrace what our waters can provide and eat more locally caught fish. Fishing has been a way of life in Newlyn for generations and we are proud to be part of that rich heritage."

With over 100 years in the fishing industry, we know a thing or two about fish. Stevenson is a family fishing business in the town of Newlyn, just outside Penzance down in the far south west of Cornwall. The Cornish fishing industry is extremely diverse, and the coastal waters here are abundant with a rich variety of fish. It is not unusual for the fish market to have 35 different species, all fresh and responsibly sourced, landed daily.

We have one of the largest privately owned fleets in Britain which catch, land and sell the finest fresh fish. Having our own fleet of boats allows us to control the entire process, from catch to customer. We are pleased to be one of the few companies that can truly say this, and with careful handling throughout the process, we can ensure our customers get the highest quality fish and shellfish every time. We also work closely with Cornish and national governing bodies to support new fishing methods. We passionately believe that it is of paramount importance to our industry that we all work together to secure long term sustainable fishing practices.

Stevenson is proud to have the first female Master Fishmonger, Elaine Lorys, running the fishmongers in Newlyn: "I've worked at Stevenson's for more than 24 years now and loved every minute of it! To do my job, you need a wide knowledge of everything to do with the fishing industry and sustainability, as well as filleting methods. I work in the shop, preparing the products and serving customers. From there, I can see our boats through the window and the fish market is about 100 feet away; it doesn't get much fresher than that!"

Stevenson's boats land species such as megrim, locally known as Cornish sole, plaice, monkfish, sardines, hake, dover and lemon sole. In the UK we have such a wealth of high quality British fish; we should all embrace what our waters can provide and eat more locally caught fish. Fishing has been a way of life in Newlyn for generations and we are proud to be part of that rich heritage. We will continue fishing, providing employment for the next generation, and working with the Newlyn community to build an even stronger industry for the future. Our mission is to ensure that the high quality, fresh Cornish fish landed by our boats is a staple on every family's weekly menu, now and in the future.

TRADITIONAL NEWLYN HAKE AND ONIONS

This is a very Cornish dish that can all be done in one pan. Hake is a delicate, very versatile fish that is traditionally eaten in Newlyn, fresh off the boats, with caramelised onions and a good dollop of buttery mashed potato. – Elaine Lorys, Master Fishmonger

2 tbsp Cornish rapeseed oil

2 medium or large white onions, sliced

2 Cornish hake loin fillets, skin on

1 lemon, halved

1 bag of samphire, washed

Sea salt and black pepper

Coat the bottom of a frying pan with a tablespoon of the rapeseed oil and place on a medium-high heat until the oil is shimmering. Add the sliced onions and stir to coat them with oil. Reduce the heat and stir occasionally as they cook. After 10 minutes, sprinkle the onions with salt and then leave them to caramelise for 30 minutes. Add a little water to the pan if the onions look like they are drying out.

Sprinkle the skin of the hake fillets with sea salt and black pepper, then rub in the seasoning to help it crisp up the skin. Heat the remaining tablespoon of rapeseed oil in a clean frying pan.

Once the pan is hot, put the hake loins skin side down into the frying pan. Gently press down with a fish slice so the fillets don't curl up. Let the hake cook for 3 minutes and then turn it over to cook on the white side. Squeeze some lemon juice over the top.

Add your caramelised onion and the washed samphire to the frying pan to cook with the hake for the final minute. Once the fish is cooked through, add another squeeze of lemon juice.

Serve the hake fillets on top of buttery mash or potato cakes (or anything else you wish to serve it with) along with the caramelised onions and samphire.

PREPARATION TIME: 5 MINUTES | COOKING TIME: 35 MINUTES | SERVES 2

Dunstanburgh Castle © Tim Green

DIRECTORY

A Fishy Business
Custom House Quay
Union Street
Salcombe
TQ8 8BZ
Telephone: 07921 551421
Instagram: @afishybusiness1
Fish and seafood store with live lobster and crabs to pick your own out of the tanks, as well as super fresh fish and live or frozen bait.

A Passion For Seafood Ltd
Website: www.apassionforseafood.com
Instagram and Facebook: @apassionforseafood
Twitter: @PassionSeafood
Artisan fish sellers, supplying seasonal British fish and shellfish direct from UK day boats to London fishmongers and chefs. We also have our own pop-up fish stall once a week.

Amy O'Brien
Instagram: @amy_andthe_sea
Female fisherman based in Newlyn, Cornwall.

Bally Philp
Telephone: 07861668806
Email: ballycroft@btinternet.com
I have been a fisherman for over 30 years, mostly working a creel boat from the Isle of Skye and landing Scottish shellfish at Kyleakin Harbour.

Câr-Y-Môr
Solva Farm
Panteg Road, Solva
Haverfordwest, Pembrokeshire
SA62 6TN
Telephone: 07772597776
Website: carymor.wales / www.solvaseafoods.co.uk
Email: admin@carymor.wales
Instagram: @car_y_mor or Facebook: @CarYMorWales
Community benefit society that started the first trial ocean farms in Wales. We have recently joined forces with Solva Seafoods which allows us to market and distribute locally caught seafood and shellfish to both local and national customers.

Colman's Fish and Chips
182-186 Ocean Road
South Shields
NE33 2JQ

Colman's Seafood Temple
Sea Road
South Shields
NE33 2LD
Telephone: 01914561202 / 01915111349
Website: www.colmansfishandchips.co.uk / www.colmansseafoodtemple.co.uk
Email: info@colmansseafoodtemple.co.uk
Social media: @colmansseafoodtemple
Sustainable seafood and fish and chip restaurants.

Cornish Seaweed
Lower Quay
Gweek
TR12 6UD
Cornwall
Telephone: 01326 618469
Website: www.cornishseaweed.co.uk
Email: info@cornishseaweed.co.uk / sales@cornishseaweed.co.uk
Social media: #cornishseaweed (for recipes, updates and competitions)
Sustainably hand harvesting a delicious range of organic Cornish seaweeds for use in everyday cooking.

Dee Caffari MBE
Website: www.deecaffari.com
Dee Caffari is a British sailor, and was the first woman to sail solo and non-stop in both directions around the globe.

E. Ashton (Fishmongers) Ltd
Central Market
Cardiff
CF10 1AU
Telephone: 02920 229 201
Website: www.ashtonfishmongers.co.uk
Family-run business selling quality fish, shellfish, game and exotic meats at one of the largest fish retail outlets in the UK.

Fairlass Shellfish Ltd & Saoirse Shellfish Ltd
Wells-next-the-Sea
Norfolk
Telephone: 07920 709732
Email: fairlassshellfish@outlook.com /
saoirseshellfish@outlook.com
Instagram: @the.female.fisherman
Female fisherman supplying crabs, lobsters and whelks.

Fisherman's Friends
Website: www.thefishermansfriends.com
Twitter: @fishy_friends
Facebook: fishermansfriends
Fisherman's Friends Management: www.mightyvillage.com
*The Fisherman's Friends have been singing traditional 'songs of
the sea' for more than 30 years in Port Isaac. They have since
signed a record deal, performed all over the UK and have a
feature film all about them with a sequel on the way!*

Flying Fish Seafoods
Old School Industrial Park
Moorland Road
Indian Queens
St. Columb
Cornwall
TR9 6JP
Telephone: 01726 862 876
Website: www.flyingfishseafoods.co.uk
Email: sales@flyingfishseafoods.co.uk
Instagram: @flyingfish525
Fine fish from ship to plate in 48.

Fresh From The Boat Ltd
Unit 2 Far Curlews
Emsworth Yacht Harbour
Thorney Road
Emsworth
PO10 8BW
Telephone: 01243 379732
Website: www.freshfromtheboat.co.uk
Email: freshfromtheboat@gmail.com
Social media: @freshfromtheboat
A local, sustainable way to buy fresh fish!

JCS Fish Limited
Murray Street
Fish Docks
Grimsby
DN31 3RD
Telephone: 01472 355217
Website: www.bigfish.co.uk / www.jcsfish.co.uk
Facebook and Instagram: @bigfishbrand
*Based in Grimsby, family-owned JCS Fish is the UK's most
experienced salmon specialist and producer of the responsibly
sourced and award-winning BigFish™ range.*

Kames Fish Farming Limited
Kames Bay
Kilmelford
Oban
PA34 4XA
Telephone: 01852 200286
Email: fish@kames.co.uk
Website: kames.co.uk
Social media: @kamesfishfarm
*Oldest family-run fish farm in Scotland, producing Scottish
steelhead trout in freshwater lochs and the sea.*

L. Robson and Sons Ltd
Haven Hill
Craster
Alnwick
Northumberland
NE66 3TR
Telephone: 01665 576 223
Website: www.kipper.co.uk
Email: sales@kipper.co.uk
*Fourth generation family business specialising in the traditional
method of oak-smoking kippers and salmon.*

The Magpie Café
14 Pier Road
Whitby
YO21 3PU

The Whitby Catch
1 Pier Rd
Whitby
YO21 3PT
Telephone: 01947 602058
Website: magpiecafe.co.uk
Email: info@magpiecafe.co.uk / www.thewhitbycatch.co.uk
Twitter: @themagpiecafe
Facebook: MagpieCafe
Harbourside fish and seafood restaurant, and fishmongers selling locally landed crabs and lobsters as well as Whitby fish and oven-ready meals.

Marine Stewardship Council
1-3 Snow Hill
Marine House
London
EC1A 2DH
Telephone: 020 7246 8900
Website: www.msc.org
Email: info@msc.org / mscintheuk@msc.org
Twitter: @MSCintheUK @MSCecolabel
Instagram: @mscintheuk @mscecolabel
Facebook: MSCintheUK / MSCecolabel
The Marine Stewardship Council is an independent non-profit organisation which sets a standard for sustainable fishing.

Mark McGorrin
Website: www.greatbritishfish.com
Instagram: @greatbritfish
Chief mate on Kirkella, the UK's leading freezer trawler catching cod and haddock in northern distant waters for the nation's fish and chip shops.

Mel Shand
Telephone: 01330850674
Website: melshand.com
Email: melshand.artist@gmail.com
Facebook and Instagram: @melshandartist
Artist, communicator, gamekeeper's wife and Trustee of the River Dee.

Michael Wright
Cruising Yachtsman
Falmouth, Cornwall
Email: wright2michael@hotmail.com
Since 2012, Michael has regularly cruised the UK and Irish coasts for extended periods.

The National Lobster Hatchery
South Quay
Padstow
Cornwall PL28 8BL
Telephone: 01841 533877
Website: www.nationallobsterhatchery.co.uk
Email: clare@nationallobsterhatchery.co.uk
Social media: @padstowlobster
A pioneering marine conservation, research and education charity and visitor education centre based in Padstow.

Pembrokeshire Scallops
1 Colby Cottage
Llawhaden
Narberth
Pembrokeshire
SA678DZ
Telephone: 07939981635
Website: www.pembrokeshirescallops.co.uk
Email: info@pembrokeshirescallops.co.uk
Facebook: PembrokeshireScallops
The finest diver-caught Welsh scallops. One is never enough!

Pengelly's Famous Fishmongers
The Quay
East Looe
Cornwall
PL13 1DX
Telephone: 01503 262246
Website: www.pengellys.co.uk
Facebook and Instagram: @pengelleysfishmongerslooe
Pengelly's Fishmongers is situated perfectly on the quayside in Looe and is famous for its quality day boat fish and shellfish.

Rachel Green
Website: www.rachel-green.co.uk
Email: info@rachel-green.co.uk
Professional chef and Seafish ambassador, championing sustainability and British seafood.

Richard Haward's Oysters Ltd
129 Coast Road
West Mersea
Essex
CO5 8PA
Telephone: 01206 382149
Website: richardhawardsoysters.shop
Email: richardhawardsoysters@gmail.com
Instagram: @richardhawardsoysters
Twitter: @rhawardoysters
Facebook: rhoysters
Richard Haward's Oysters is an oyster retailer in Essex, and one of the oldest oyster farming families in the world.

Royal National Lifeboat Institution (RNLI)
West Quay Road
Poole
Dorset
BH15 1HZ
Telephone: 0300 300 9990
Website: rnli.org
Email: supportercare@rnli.org.uk
Social media: @RNLI
The charity that saves lives at sea. Since 1824, our lifeboat crews and lifeguards have saved more than 140,000 lives.

Royal Navy
Website: royalnavy.mod.uk/careers/catering
Being a caterer in the Royal Navy is a career that is literally miles from anything you could do at home. Travelling around the world, your job will range from cooking for the ship's company on board warships or Royal Marines on land operations, to serving a fine dining experience to politically influential VIPs and royalty.

Scottish Association for Marine Science (SAMS)
Dunbeg
By Oban
Argyll
Scotland
PA37 1QA
Telephone: 01631 559000
Website: www.sams.ac.uk
Email: info@sams.ac.uk
Twitter: @SAMSoceannews
Instagram: @SAMSmarinescience
Facebook: SAMS.Marine
LinkedIn: samsmarinescience
SAMS has been delivering independent marine science since 1884. Based in Oban, 160 staff are working for healthy and sustainably managed seas and oceans through world-class marine research, education and engagement with society.

Scottish Shellfish
1 Pit Road
Belgrave Street
Motherwell Food Park
Bellshill
ML4 3NZ
Telephone: 01698 844221
Website: https://www.scottishshellfish.co.uk
Email: shellfish@scottishshellfish.co.uk
Social media: @ScottishShellfish
Co-operative with farms across mainland Scotland and the Shetland Isles, producing shellfish including mussels, oysters, brown crab, giant scallops and Maine lobster.

Seafish
18 Logie Mill
Logie Green Road
Edinburgh
EH7 4HS
Website: www.seafish.org
Twitter: @seafishuk

Love Seafood
Website: www.loveseafood.co.uk
Social media: @loveseafooduk
Seafish aims to give the UK seafood sector the support it needs to thrive. It's a non-departmental public body using a unique, non-competitive position to work in partnership with businesses, government and organisations to overcome challenges and seize opportunities. Love Seafood is brought to you by Seafish and is an ambitious 20 year initiative which brings together seafood champions to inform and inspire the nation to enjoy a better, more balanced lifestyle.

The Seafood Shack
West Argyle Street
Ullapool
IV26 2TY
Telephone: 07876142623 / 07596722846
Email: theseafoodshack@hotmail.com
Website: www.seafoodshack.co.uk
Catering trailer offering fresh and local seafood cooked to order from the area's finest produce.

Sole Bay Fish Company Limited
22E Blackshore
Ferry Road
Southwold
Suffolk
IP18 6ND
Telephone: 01502 724241
Email: solebayfishco@gmail.com
Fresh locally caught fish and shellfish from our boats, simply prepared, cooked and presented.

South West Coast 700
Website: swc700.com
The website is an essential guide for all those looking to plan a trip on the south west coast and provides information on the routes, places to stay, things to do, places to visit, things to see, experiences, attractions, places to eat and buy food.

Star Castle Hotel
St Mary's
Isles of Scilly
TR21 0JA
Website: www.star-castle.co.uk
Telephone: 01720 422317
Instagram, Twitter and Facebook: @starcastlehotel
Family-run hotel with breath-taking views and award-winning food including fresh lobster and crab caught by the hotel owner's very own boat.

The Urban Fishwife
Caroline Rye
Website: www.theurbanfishwife.com
Email: caroline@theurbanfishwife.com
Instagram: @urbanfishwife
Recipes from the city, stories from the sea: food writing, recipe development, food styling and consultancy focusing on sustainable seafood.

Vin Sullivan Foods
2 Gilchrist Thomas Ind Est
Blaenavon
Gwent
NP4 9RL
Telephone: 01495 792792
Website: vinsullivan.com / www.fishshack.co.uk
Fine food supplier with fresh fish and seafood available online from The Fish Shack, at the mobile fishmonger's stall on market days in Abergavenny and Pontypridd, and from the shop in Blaenavon.

Wester Ross Fisheries Ltd
Ardmair
Ullapool
Wester Ross
Scotland
IV26 2TN
Website: www.wrs.co.uk
For home deliveries: www.osprey.scot
Wester Ross is the oldest owner-operated premium salmon
farmer in the UK, situated in the Scottish Highlands, hand-
rearing superior all-natural, medicine-free Scottish salmon.

W. Stevenson & Sons
Harbour Offices
Newlyn
Penzance
Cornwall
TR18 5HB
Telephone: 01736 362998
Website: wstevenson.co.uk
Historic family fishing business in the village of Newlyn, and the
home of Cornwall's only Master Fishmonger, Elaine Lorys.